In Search of the **Church**

New Testament Images for Tomorrow's Congregations

Keith A. Russell

An Alban Institute Publication

The Publications Program of The Alban Institute is assisted by a grant from Trinity Church, New York City.

Library of Congress Catalog Card Number 93-74583
ISBN 1-56699-123-4

*Dedicated to Marian Ronan,
my partner and wife.*

CONTENTS

Preface   vii

I. Introduction: In Search of the Church   1

II. Mark: An Alternative Community   11

III. Matthew: Households of Justice   23

IV. Luke: Signs of the Kingdom   38

V. Paul: Communities of Reconciliation   52

VI. 1 Peter: Homes for the Homeless   65

VII. The Apocalypse of John: Communities of Resistance   79

VIII. In Search of the Church: An Invitation   95

Notes   105

PREFACE

This book is written to and for congregations as they struggle to make sense of the current crisis in the church. What shall we do about our decline? What can be done to reverse what appears to be a downward spiral? Can we chart a new future and find solutions to problems now before us? It is my deep conviction that congregations are capable of the kind of change necessary to understand the present situation and to begin construction of a new and different future.

I have sought to bring to the discussion of the church's current situation the insights of contemporary biblical scholarship. What do scholars say about the formation of the church in the New Testament era, and can those insights enable us in the last decade of the twentieth century to have a new and perhaps different dialogue about our life in congregations? Because congregations often do not have access to the work of biblical scholars, I have sought here to make recent New Testament scholarship on ecclesiology available for our consideration. I believe that biblical scholarship can be an important gift to us in congregations as we seek to consider our future.

In Search of the Church is a study book for use in settings such as adult classes, new member classes, leadership training events, and retreats. Questions for discussion and reflection accompany each chapter. Chapter 8 presents a more detailed planning process for those who want to take this material and turn it into an action plan for one or more aspects of congregational life.

All of this is offered out of twin convictions. First, congregations are capable of change, even radical change, that will produce new life now and begin the process of moving toward a reconceived future.

Second, a fresh consideration of images of the church in the New Testament will help us with this task of congregational redevelopment.

CHAPTER I

Introduction:
In Search of the Church

Congregational Problems Today

If you are concerned about the condition of congregations in our time, I
invite you to join me in thinking about our current status and in asking
where we are going in the church. I invite you to undertake with me a
search for the church in the present by means of a search for the church
in the past. More specifically, are there images of the church in our past
that might be beneficial for our present struggle?

We cannot deny that congregations today struggle to cope with some
very difficult problems. Declining membership, scarce resources, and
increasing costs all suggest that we are losing influence in our society.
The majority of church congregations in the U.S. have a membership of
fewer than one hundred members. More and more of them face the
reality that they can no longer afford full-time professional leadership.
The rising cost of medical insurance and pensions alone make it less and
less possible for small congregations to afford full-time, seminary-
trained leadership.

Even as we attempt to cope with these intracongregational difficulties, our world itself is in crisis. People are in pain in both urban and
rural settings. Poverty, unemployment, hunger, and homelessness are all
increasing. We face the prospect that for the first time in our nation's
history, the current generation of young people will be less financially
secure and have fewer opportunities than did their parents and their
grandparents. Our search for the church is not being conducted in a
secure and stable time. In fact, the time in which we seek to find our
way is troubled as the church is troubled.

As a result of these circumstances, many in congregations are worried or disheartened. It's hard to know what to do next. Some have even stopped hoping for anything better. Many, clergy and laity alike, seem to have lost the ability to imagine a new and better future. All this notwithstanding, we are suspicious of the quick-fix solutions marketed to solve our problems. It is hard to believe that leadership training at the Crystal Cathedral, a new evangelism program, or the latest technique in strategic planning will bring about the changes that we intuitively know our congregations need.

Over twenty-five years, as I have worked to understand the nature of the problems facing congregations, I have been drawn again and again to the New Testament. It is clear to me that the hints we find in the New Testament about the developing church in the first century can be a source of real help for us as we move toward the twenty-first century. Yet turning to the New Testament for help in our search for the contemporary church requires that we recognize what we do not find there; there are no blueprints to be copied. The New Testament is by no means a manual on how to develop or organize the church.

When we go in search of the exciting yet little-explored church in the New Testament, we are confronted with diverse and sometimes conflicting images of what the church is and what it does. Depending on where we look, we see different things. The New Testament is filled with portraits of various communities in formation. Where the community is forming, when it is forming, and what the world around it is like makes a great difference in the kind of community we find, the image of the church that we discover there.

One way to explain these differences is to say that the New Testament church is incarnational. The body of Christ that emerges in Antioch is not the same as its partners in Rome, in Philippi, or in Asia Minor. As a matter of fact, even churches in different parts of one geographical area prove dissimilar in look or outlook. Paul and other New Testament writers accurately portray the conflict in and among congregations in the first century. Incarnation can be messy.

In spite of, or perhaps even because of, this incarnational messiness, we can discern primary pictures or images of the church throughout the New Testament. In the pages that follow, I seek to sketch out these primary images of the church as they are found in the books of Mark, Matthew, Luke, Peter, and John of the Apocalypse, and in Paul's letters.

The New Testament is a rich mosaic of images and pictures of the emerging church each with interesting implications for the journeys facing congregations in our time. For us to use this mosaic effectively, we must explore some common characteristics that cut across the various New Testament communities.

Common Characteristics of New Testament Churches

Of the several characteristics that emerging New Testament churches have in common, the first we will consider is that these communities were organized in households.[1] The household was the basic organizing structure of the Roman Empire, and the church took the household as its own form for more than four centuries. This factor has gone relatively unexamined by scholars until recently.

What was a Roman household? It was much broader and more extended than the nuclear family as we understand it. It was more like a large extended family of aunts, uncles, cousins, hired hands, and servants; it included even animals and other possessions.

There were two different kinds of households in the Roman Empire. The primary model of household was the *paterfamilias*, that is, an extended family under the direction and domination of males, a patriarchal, hierarchical structure. Another model of the household, however, was the *collegia*; these were more voluntary societies formed for the purposes of trade, vocation, or community benefit. *Collegia* were larger than the *paterfamilias* and more egalitarian. The Greek word for household, *oikos*, as used in the New Testament can mean *paterfamilias* or *collegia*.

There is a significant tension in the New Testament between these two models of household. We will see that the New Testament church is not solely based on paternal hierarchy. The head of the church household is not the resident male but Jesus Christ. The New Testament household seems to struggle for equality and to honor the reality that in Christ there is neither Greek nor Jew, bond nor free, male nor female (Gal. 3:28). It would appear that the early Christians sought to convert the traditional pattern of social organization, the *paterfamilias*, to fit its more revolutionary and inclusive theological perspective, and this battle is reflected in the pages of the New Testament.

The households organized in response to the reality of Jesus Christ were often multilingual, multicultural, and from the very beginning they included the rich and the poor. We also know that women exercised significant leadership in many of these new communities. The households provided a foundation for communal growth, were the locus of cultic activities such as the Eucharist, and undergirded economic sharing. Households met at sites accommodating ten to twenty people to larger sites that could hold thirty, fifty, and even a hundred. In adopting the household as its form, the early church provided the convert with a new and primary community to which to belong, a community clearly intended to replace the primary community from which the convert came.

New Testament churches had a second factor in common: They were sectarian.[2] The emerging church was not a subset of the dominant culture. Its dramatic growth did not come about because it was favored or protected by the state. It was not a tax-exempt, not-for-profit organization. It was a sect existing on the edge of Roman society, often outside societal laws and mores, or at least substantially at odds with them.

Recent scholarship suggests that sects have a number of typical characteristics and that New Testament churches exhibited most or all of them. Like sects in general, New Testament churches emerged out of protest. Allegiance to Jesus was a choice over and against other dominant realities; to join this new movement was to place yourself in tension with the dominant culture and its values. The early church rejected the reality claimed or taken for granted by the political and religious establishment. "Blessed are the poor" was not a primary societal value, but it was a primary organizing tenet of the churches. They rejected the culture of privilege and power and invited the exile, the alien, the slave and the master, the widow, and the orphan to find a new reality in Jesus the Christ and a new social community in the church.

In taking this new social and religious posture, the early churches were also remarkably egalitarian in organization. Many of the disagreements reflected in the Pauline epistles were fights over the implications of this new freedom. The early church grew rapidly in part because, like other sects, it offered its adherents love and acceptance within the community; that is, the church became a primary place of belonging in urban areas in a time of severe social dislocation. The households of faith were mostly located in urban areas, centers of migration. The church provided a welcoming home and place of acceptance for aliens, exiles, and displaced people from all over the Roman Empire. It was a new family and a new community that claimed a new unity in response to Christ.

Membership in these new communities was totally voluntary. You had to choose to align yourself with this new movement to receive the benefits and privileges it offered. If you did join, the church sought total commitment of your life and resources. Sects do not want your spare time or your spare change. They want you. The early churches reflected this reality; the movement sought the total commitment of its members.

The New Testament households both constructed and provided an alternative social reality to which people could belong. Conversion to Jesus was a conversion to a new community that, although marginal and fragile, promised a new sense of self and a new sense of purpose. Sects tend to be on the margins, but they offer what the dominant culture often prohibits or discourages. The New Testament households offered acceptance to the marginal, became a home for exiles and aliens, and provided a new way of perceiving the reality of the world. Salvation in Christ meant throwing your lot in with a new group that offered in return love, acceptance, and a new lease on life. Being in Christ was not so much a private personal experience as it was a personal experience in and with a new social structure—the church.

Early churches had a third common characteristic: They were eschatological in their point of view; a shared focus on the future cut across all locations and organizational structures. The early churches had a vision of the future that empowered the present and gave hope to the believer, and the eschatology that informed them was often apocalyptic.

Apocalyptic is a term referring to any prophetic revelation of the future; the early Christian revelation stressed a battle between good and evil and required from its members an active resistance to evil. As we will see in our consideration of John's Revelation, New Testament apocalypticism was often related to political resistance. The early church may have been far more politically involved than we have been led to believe. To be in the church was to align yourself with a community and a set of values that were basically in conflict with Rome and its values. "Jesus is Lord," one of the earliest communal affirmations of faith, was both profoundly theological and deeply political. If Jesus Christ was Lord, then Caesar could not be. As we shall see, early Christians often were troubled, harassed, and sometimes persecuted for making this confessional claim.

Apocalypticism was a way of asking, "Who is in charge of history and who controls the ending or outcome of time?" The New Testament perspective affirmed that God was the final authority, God would act, and in the last analysis God would be faithful to God's promises. This perspective sought to explain evil, demystify its power, and fire the socio-political imagination of the believer to resist current oppressors for the sake of ultimate victory and vindication. Apocalypticism described the nature of evil while it painted vivid portraits of the future that God had in store (see Rev. 21). The symbolic visions and wild images characteristic of apocalyptic literature were intended to keep the pressure on the believer to live as if the present situation were not the primary or final reality. The believer was invited to dream dreams, have visions, and see beyond what is to what might lie ahead at the end of time.

Across the households of faith in the New Testament, the discipline of seeing the future was critical to understanding and living in the present. The future was an instrument for interpreting the present and was instructive for faith and action. Through this process the churches of the New Testament engaged in eschatological thinking. These sectarian households existed as an alternative in their time in large part because they could see beyond that time while not abandoning the age in which God had placed them. The future that God had in store for the believer and the world shaped the believers' response to their world and gave them a power to survive, thrive, and, when necessary, resist.

Eschatological Thinking

As we shall see, all three of the characteristics common to the developing churches in the New Testament have implications for our consideration of contemporary congregations. In each of the New Testament books or letters examined in these pages, we will be faced with the question of community and culture. In all cases the churches are households that seek and struggle to form a new social commitment and structure in their time. Likewise, throughout the New Testament we will find households on the edge of or in conflict with their society. In our search for the church, we will wrestle frequently with the implications of both community and sectarian marginality.

It strikes me, however, that we have much to gain from a more in-depth consideration of the third characteristic of New Testament communities: eschatological thinking. As a matter of fact, this work is itself an invitation to the reader to engage in eschatological thinking. If we are to achieve our goal, if we are to be successful in our search for the church of today, we must recover a vision of hope as it pertains to tomorrow, to the future. We must recover an ability to imagine a new future, to conceive alternatives that are more than our present and transcend our past. Our loss of this ability to imagine a new and viable future is at the center of the crisis we currently face in congregations.

We could become a new community of believers if we could see beyond what *is* to what *might be*. If we could recover our ability to envision the future, we might be able to transform the present. Eschatology is a vision of tomorrow not so that we can escape the present but so that we can live in the present with a passion and confidence that transcends it. As we look carefully at the developing church in the New Testament, we realize that we have a lot to learn about thinking eschatologically.

There is, of course, a great deal that hinders us from thinking eschatologically. In many of our congregations we are preoccupied with how things used to be as a way of avoiding our current pain and unhappiness. We have lost hope, so we look back and glory in what used to be; in truth, very often we don't like the present, but we have nothing to substitute for it. We cling to what we have lost and act defeated and depressed.

Glorifying the past can never be the key to our future. We need to get a new perspective on today by getting a new vision of tomorrow. We are stuck with the misery of the moment unless we can see beyond the now, unless we can be apprehended by the power of "the not yet." If we can see the new, we can become new. A fresh and powerful vision of the future would help us think differently about the present.

We turn to the New Testament in search of a vision of the church that transcends our current pessimism and empowers us to lift our weary eyes to focus not on all that is wrong but on what might transform the now and enable us to hope again. When we think about the future that God has in store for us, we must help one another to see a new day coming where pain and sorrow have been transformed, where greed and grime do not predominate, where race and culture are not sources of division but an opportunity for unity. When we can see what might be, we will not have to settle for the mess that is around us. Thinking eschatologically can lift our spirits, sharpen our focus, and empower our protest.

A Parable of Possibility

The creation of communities like those found in the New Testament is possible today. We know that because from time to time we see just such communities springing up among us. I am reminded of a community that New York Theological Seminary, an interdenominational seminary in New York City, has sponsored for the last ten years at Sing Sing prison.

Sing Sing is a maximum-security facility, and the community is a master's level theological training program for long-term prisoners. Every year twelve to fifteen men from various prisons around New York State are accepted into the program and transferred to Sing Sing to engage in an intensive one-year training program to prepare for various aspects of prison ministry. These men come together out of a desire to be ministers; to do this, they must learn how to work together, pray together, and live together.

Year after year, the long-term prisoners in this program become a sectarian and eschatological community within the prison. The overall environment in which the community is formed is violent and negative; furthermore, some guards and officials are overtly hostile to the program, and other prisoners ridicule it. To overcome this, the men must find a picture of the future that enables them to make sense of the present and hold on to hope.

In effect, these extraordinary students are forced to find a new unity, a community, based not simply on what they have in common but on what they are becoming in Christ. While carrying out such a task is difficult, the seminary has discovered that it is both possible and compelling. There are now more than one hundred graduates spread across prisons in New York State, serving as assistants to chaplains or assisting in other social ministries and helping to set up other small communities of faith and hope. The graduates of the program become the leaders of these faith communities out of their own experience of eschatological, sectarian community. In so doing they help to provide an alternative to despair and destruction and enable others to dream new dreams and have saving hope.

If it is possible to build communities of faith and hope in as difficult a place as Sing Sing prison, think what could be accomplished in contemporary congregations. Like the prisoners at Sing Sing, men and women today long for something that transcends their hates, overcomes their despair, and engages them in the ability to hope and sing again. Many people are in search of the church, in search of community.

Perhaps what the church has to offer in this troubled time is precisely a form of life where alternatives to hate and violence, greed and destruction can be envisioned, where life can be celebrated for what it might be rather than denounced for what it is not. I believe that many of us in congregations today hunger for such a community and are searching for more. Let us continue together this search for the church, believing that if we see beyond what is, we can become what we yearn to be.

Questions and Exercises for Further Study

1. Read aloud the following examples of eschatological thinking in the New Testament: Luke 4:16-21; 2 Corinthians 4:7-18; Revelation 21:1-6. What visions of the future do you find portrayed in these passages? Which do you find most compelling?

2. By yourself or in a group, spend ten minutes in silence trying to imagine a new heaven and a new earth like the one described in Revelation 21. What picture emerges from this reading for you? What does it make you feel? After the period of silence, come together as a group and discuss what you experienced. After each person has a chance to describe his or her picture, discuss any similarities and differences among the impressions. Discuss anything that seems important.

3. What kind of future would you like? In answering this question, consider concrete aspects of your life and personality: Where you live, how you spend your time, what aspects of the world make you happy or cause you to worry. Spend about five minutes thinking about this. Then discuss with others the qualities or characteristics of the future that you have just been imagining. If you had a different vision of your future, how might it affect the changes you would make in your life?

4. What kind of help would you need from your congregation to be able to think more about the future in this way? Are there things you need to study? How does worship help or hinder your approach to the future?

5. In what ways is your congregation like a New Testament household? In what ways is it different?

6. In what ways, if any, could you characterize your congregation as sectarian? What are the signs of this? Do you think there needs to be more tension between your congregation and the larger society? Explain.

Mark:
An Alternative Community

Social Setting and Historical Context

Mark, the first of the gospels to be written, was composed in the second
generation of the Christian church in Northern Palestine, around 66 C.E.[1]
At this time the households of faith about which Mark was concerned
still understood themselves as a sect within Judaism; as such, they were
caught, with the rest of Palestinian Jewry, in the middle of a severe social
and political crisis. Mark's record of Jesus' life, death, and resurrection
was aimed at trying to help these small households come to terms with
the demands and dangers of their times while they sought to be faithful
to the teachings of the Nazarene named Jesus.

In 66 C.E. Palestine was under Roman occupation. Different
groups within Palestinian society were responding in different ways to
the reality of military occupation, and Mark's community was under
considerable pressure to adopt one of these strategies.

First of all, there was the Jewish elite, consisting of the high priestly
families and the Sadducees who sought to keep the peace by cooperating
with the Roman authorities. This group believed that it was better to
compromise than to lose what autonomy remained to them.

Second, there were the Pharisees who opposed this collaboration
and called for reform within Judaism itself. The Pharisees were in many
ways the "liberals" in this struggle; they wanted to reform and purify
religious leadership and practice rather than overthrow or destroy it.[2]

A third group, the Essenes, called for withdrawal from all current
practices and alliances and the development of separate communities.
The primarily monastic vision of the Essenes was critical of Jewish

collaborators and Roman colonialists alike but lacked any real strategy of engagement.[3] Like the Pharisees, the Essenes were more interested in purging the dominant order than in overthrowing it.

A fourth group, the Zealots, called for a direct break with Rome, an end to collaboration, and armed insurrection. For some time, the Zealots had been engaging in attacks on Roman and Jewish leaders and on the symbols of both establishments. They wanted to rid themselves of Rome and of the ruling priestly leadership. Eventually their political and military resistance provoked a major and bloody response by Rome, culminating in the destruction of the Temple in 70 C.E.

In his gospel, Mark seeks to delineate a path for his households to follow through this upheaval. He does not counsel collaboration, reform, withdrawal, or overthrow. Instead, he presents his households with another picture, one that challenges them to take up an alternative stance within the current situation. Mark calls this small sect, which has been struggling to carve out an identity within Judaism or beyond it, to refuse to take sides. Mark calls it to adopt a nonaligned stance based on belief in a new world order to be accomplished through the practice of radical discipleship.[4]

For Mark, such discipleship comes about through the cross, the symbol of Jesus' victory over the powers of death and domination. Mark calls the Christians in Palestine to be an alternative community with the cross of Jesus as their symbol of resistance. An affirmative response to this call to become nonaligned communities of resistance meant that the struggling Christian community became an object of criticism or condemnation by those on all sides of the crisis. We will benefit by exploring in greater depth this call by Mark to the households of faith to stand alone in the midst of crisis and upheaval as disciples of the cross.

Exploring Mark's Image of the Church

Mark's gospel is full of action. Its story is built around a structure of mission, journey, and conflict. The style of writing employed in this gospel communicates a sense of urgency. It is strongly influenced by Jewish apocalyptic literature, a form of communication commonly used in Mark's time for the expression of political protest. For Mark, the apocalyptic is at the center of the story of Jesus' life, teaching, miracles, and conflicts culminating in the cross.

Mark tells the story of Jesus in such a way that requires a clear choice between good and evil. Through the depiction in his gospel of the radical dualism between good and evil, Mark conveys to his followers that a showdown with the forces of domination and evil is utterly inevitable. The parable of the strong man's house (Mark 3:22-27) illustrates this confrontation with "the powers" and indicates that Jesus is going to engage in a direct action against them.

Jesus tells this parable in response to the religious leadership accusing him of being evil, a representative of Satan. Jesus responds that Satan cannot clean out his own house (3:23), suggesting that it remains to Jesus to lead a revolt against the powers and bring their rule to an end (3:26). Jesus is going to bind the strong man and plunder his house for the sake of the new age, the coming kingdom. The followers of Mark are charged with a similar task. They too must combat the "strong men," the evil powers of their age.[5]

The story is also communicated as if it were a secret revelation. Jesus counsels his followers to keep his identity secret, but his disciples consistently fail to grasp the meaning of this request. Right up to the very end they fail to "get the message."

The message was difficult for them to comprehend in part at least because it claims that suffering is the means to the disempowerment of evil, the primary strategy for "binding the strong man." For Mark the cross represents the victory of God over the forces of evil. When Jesus dies, the powers are pulled from the highest places. The disciples are to take up their crosses and follow Jesus in the same nonviolent manner and with the same expectation of apocalyptic victory.

With this apocalyptic framework in mind, the gospel can be outlined as follows:[6]

NARRATIVE THEME	BOOK 1	BOOK 2
A. Prologue/Call to Discipleship	1:1-20	8:27-9:13
B. Campaign of Direct Action	1:21-3:35	11:1-13:3
C. Construction of New Order	4:35-8:10	8:22-26; 9:14-10:52

NARRATIVE THEME	BOOK 1	BOOK 2
D. Extended Sermon	4:1-34	13:4-37
E. Passion Tradition	6:14-29	14:1-15:38
F. Symbolic Epilogue	8:11-21	15:39-16:86

The gospel of Mark is structured so that Mark makes the same point in each of his two books: Jesus is the messiah of God. This central theme is woven throughout the gospel, with an emphasis from beginning to end on the necessity of choosing Jesus. The end of Book 1 asks the believer, "Do you not yet understand?" (8:21). Book 2 begins with a related question, "Who do you say that I am?" (8:29). Mark's presentation of Jesus continually confronts the believer with the need to choose, to choose Jesus the messiah and his way of the cross.

This central story of Mark's gospel has three subplots.[7] First, Jesus attempts to create a messianic community focused on the disciples. Next, Jesus engages in a ministry of healing, exorcism, and proclamation of the kingdom of God aimed at the poor, women, and other marginal groups. Finally, Jesus confronts the powers of his age, political and religious. This confrontation results in his death.

Mark's message to the households of faith is that the struggle they are experiencing and Jesus' struggle depicted in the gospel's three subplots are one and the same. Jesus seeks to build an alternative community based on the coming reign of God and the inevitability of the cross; Mark counsels his households of faith to do the same. The extended sermons in Books 1 and 2 are aimed at helping these beleaguered Christians to stand fast and to understand this.

To illustrate this alternative lifestyle to which the households of faith are called, Mark introduces the parable of the sower (4:1-34) and the signs of the end (13:4-37). The believer is to be like the seed that falls on good soil and to wait patiently for the harvest. Likewise the Markan communities, understanding the nature of the struggle for the kingdom of God, are charged to watch and pray (13:37). Mark's presentation of Jesus is focused on encouraging the believers to stand fast in this alternative way of the cross and not to choose the way of the Romans, the Zealots, or the Pharisees.

This need to choose under pressure helps to explain why Mark is the only gospel that keeps confronting the believers with the demand that they "understand" the nature of the task before them. Or, rather, the disciples are continually accused of not understanding. The gospel makes clear, moreover, that they will not be empowered to grasp the task until Jesus has suffered death on the cross. In the final hours the disciples abandon Jesus and do not choose the way of the cross (14:66f.). Yet with the death of Jesus, Mark claims that the power of the oppressors has been overcome, giving the disciples the courage to take the route Jesus took. The resurrection, a minor theme in the gospel of Mark, is a sign that the cross is indeed the promised victory and a guarantee of the kingdom's coming.

Mark's Jesus is by no means a victim who can do nothing but suffer. The cross is not a defeat but a chosen action and response. Jesus takes the initiative to challenge the powers of his age. In effect, Mark portrays Jesus as demanding a response. From the very moment of his baptism, Jesus confronts the power and authority of religious and political leaders. As a result of this challenge, Jesus was accused of blasphemy in the healing of the paralytic (2:1-11); he was criticized for eating with sinners and tax collectors (2:15-17); and he was challenged for healing on the Sabbath (2:23-28). Already in the third chapter of this gospel, the Pharisees and the Herodians are plotting Jesus' death.

This rejection did not silence Jesus or change his behavior. Jesus continued to proclaim the coming of the kingdom of God (4:1-34), to heal the sick (5:1-43), and to confront his accusers (7:1-23). Mark is attempting to communicate to the households of faith that they, though troubled and pressured, are not to seek some easy way or follow the course of least resistance. In his portrayal of Jesus, Mark challenges his households to keep the faith, follow the course that Jesus took, and not give in to or cower before the forces surrounding them.

In a similar fashion, many of the healing narratives in Mark's gospel assure the Markan communities that they too will be healed, strengthened, forgiven, and restored if they keep their faith in Jesus. The healing of the Gerasene demoniac (5:1-20) conveys to the Markan community that no power is stronger than the power of Jesus. The demoniac named Legion is a man in so many pieces and in so much pain that it seemed no one could help him, but in the interaction with Jesus, he is healed and reclaimed.

The woman with the flow of blood (5:21-35) is likewise a story of desperate need on the part of one who counted for very little in her time.

Yet she is recognized and rewarded by Jesus: "Daughter, your faith has made you well; go in peace and be healed of your disease" (5:34). For Mark, faith is believing in Jesus in the same way that the woman with the flow of blood believed. His message to the communities of faith is that if they do as the woman did, they, too, will be healed, sustained, and empowered.

From beginning to end, Mark's invitation is to become disciples of the cross. Mark does not ask his communities to be passively resigned to bad times, nor does he expect them to be powerless or hopeless. This is not an invitation to victimization or to sacramental whining. Mark's message, while difficult, is meant to inspire hope and encourage active resistance on the part of the church in the world. The cross is put forth as a symbol of power and victory which, when taken up by the disciples, does not result in defeat but in the experience of the power of Jesus and of the reality of the kingdom that he announced.

The picture of Jesus in the gospel of Mark is not, however, one of resistance and suffering as an end in itself. The believing community is invited to resist and to choose the way that might lead to suffering for the sake of a new order. Jesus announces a new reality in which the poor, the diseased, the oppressed, women, and children have central places. Two major sections of the gospel focus on the nature and character of the kingdom of God that Jesus both inaugurates and fulfills (4:35-8:10; 9:14-10:52). The households of faith at the center of Mark's concern are challenged to form themselves in such a way that they represent something new in the world, the kingdom of God. This newness, the coming reign of God, required nothing less than resistance as the primary shape of the church's presence in Galilee in the late sixties.

As Jesus' message was urgent and dramatic, so the Markan communities lived with a sense of urgency and drama. As Jesus' message was challenged, resisted, and rejected, so the Markan communities could expect to be challenged, resisted, and rejected. Mark presented a picture in which the stakes were high and the challenge was to choose the alternative route, that of suffering resistance. Mark wanted his households to make the right choice in a very difficult time. This means a passionate plea to stand fast and not compromise or capitulate is at the heart of his message.

This depiction of Jesus and his disciples doubtless brought some comfort to the Markan households in Palestine. Peter, James, and John clearly had difficulty understanding and following Jesus, and they had known him personally. Two generations later, believers were also having difficulty understanding and keeping straight what it meant to be a follower of Jesus.

Certainly Mark's households would have found it easier to compromise with Rome or to join the Essenes in retreat. It might have been easier as well to take up arms with the Zealots. Yet Mark counsels against all these options and calls for another: nonaligned resistance for the sake of the reign of God. On the eve of Roman military intervention, in the midst of extraordinary crisis, Mark's gospel was a call not to take sides but to create an alternative, a new community, a resistance of the old for the sake of the new.

Doubtless, it was difficult to do what Mark advised. Alternative routes are hard at any time, but especially in a crisis. Mark's telling of the Jesus story is meant not only to challenge the believers to stand fast there and then, but also to offer them eschatological assurance that their faithfulness will be sustained and rewarded. The gospel begins with the baptism of Jesus (1:9-11), and that baptism is the first sign of eschatological power. The heavens open, the Spirit descends like a dove, and a voice comes from heaven, "You are my Son, the Beloved; with you I am well pleased."

The second assurance is the story of the transfiguration (9:2-8). In this event, after Jesus converses with Moses and Elijah, the heavens open and a voice says, "This is my Son, the Beloved; listen to him!"

Finally, the crucifixion is the concluding sign of apocalyptic victory (15:33-39). As at the baptism and the transfiguration, there is a change in the heavens and an announcement: "Truly this man was God's Son!"

Mark's telling of the good news of Jesus is punctuated throughout by divine intervention and confirmation. Mark seems to assure his households that, while the road may be difficult, the end is clear. Just as God's power is manifested at the beginning, the middle, and the end of Jesus' journey, so, too, could the believing community expect God's power throughout its journey. The households of faith would be encouraged and strengthened by such signs of divine intervention.

In summary, then, when we look at the gospel of Mark we see a picture of the church as a community of resistance with the cross of Jesus as its central symbol.

Let's consider now the implications of this picture for congregations in our time.

Implications of the Markan Picture of the Church

What implications does the Markan portrait of the church have for congregations today? We could use Mark's picture to help us think about a
whole range of problems and concerns currently confronting us. For
example, Mark's gospel has clear implications for stewardship, evangelism, or outreach. At this time, however, I want to consider the implications of Mark's portrait for the worship life and educational programs of
the church.

As we have seen, the households Mark addressed had a sense of
urgency about their lives—about existing, about coming together.
Pressures to make decisions and to grow into the commitment of being
Christian were clear and steady ones. Being an alternative community in
the world demanded support, discussion, celebration, and confession.
Mark's picture of the church does not leave room for individuals to go it
alone or be separate from a believing community. Without a community
in which to worship and learn, it was simply not possible to be a disciple
of the cross.

Thus, we can imagine how important worship was to Mark's households of faith. Without daily prayer and confession, how would these
communities have survived in such a frightening and hostile time? Without regular gathering for sharing fears, worries, and hopes, how could
they have stayed faithful to the task that Mark outlined? Without instruction, how could they have done what was asked? Worship played an
important role in remembering what Jesus said, how he acted, and what
he was asking in that time. Worship called people into a community that
sought to celebrate their new-found freedom and salvation and to work
out the day-to-day implications of believing. Through prayers, singing,
teaching, and the Eucharist, those early Christians sought to stay connect-
ed to one another, to God, and to the mission to which they felt called.

In contrast to this, worship in the great majority of Protestant congregations today is a one-hour-a-week experience attended by decreasing
numbers of people. Congregations have for some time now been pressed
to consolidate their work and concerns into this one-hour weekly event.
In that short space of time we try to share concerns, confess sins, receive
forgiveness, offer prayer, hear a sermon, and give our offering. If we
observe the Eucharist, then we eliminate some other item because we
believe that the service must not go over one hour.

Is it any wonder that clergy and lay expectations about the worth and power of worship are declining steadily? How can we squeeze the drama of life and death into one hour? How can we abbreviate the confession of sins and the assurance of forgiveness into a two-minute segment and have it mean anything? How can people's broken hearts, troubled relationships, ethical questions, and personal problems be taken seriously when only five minutes is allowed for prayer and even less time for reflection? More and more worship has become a professionally orchestrated, concentrated event that seeks to compress within itself an extraordinary range of the congregation's weekly needs.

What underlies this compression and tight orchestration of the worship life of congregations? Perhaps it is a reflection of a deeper and more profound problem regarding the essential nature of what the church has become in our society. The church is no longer the place where our souls are stirred, the drama of human life celebrated, or the hard questions of our lives and times confronted. Put otherwise, few contemporary Christian congregations have a Markan picture of themselves.

Mark's picture forces us to confront the lack of urgency undergirding our experience of worship. Behind our lack of urgency to gather may be our confusion about the mission of the congregation, our place in society, and the role the church actually plays in providing us with an alternative way to understand and live our lives. Perhaps we could get a new perspective on mission and role not by engaging in general discussion about what we should do but by talking honestly about why we need to worship in a time like ours.

Why might we need to gather in community to worship God? Because human beings in our community and around the world are in pain. Because we are isolated and lonely. Because we are tired of how hard life seems. Because we long to have our hope redefined. Because we need a place where it is safe to weep and be comforted. Because we want to see the future through the eyes of God. Because we face so many problems that we are growing more and more hardened and insensitive to others—and we do not like it. Because we would like to celebrate but don't quite know how. Because we want to feel God's presence and experience a peace that passes all understanding.

Could it be that worship redefined as a way of taking our condition seriously and seeking the presence of God might enable us freshly to conceive the whole mission of congregations? Many African-American churches remain vital because their worship services are aimed at touching the heart, stirring the soul, pushing the mind, and motivating response. Time is not a problem. These churches do not rush their worship experience. They make it a point to allow space for the Holy Spirit to move and for the people to respond. For similar reasons, the charismatic movement has had a significant impact on the traditional white Protestant church. Charismatics focus on the drama of God's presence and call for response to God whether in silent tears, shouts of joy, or ecstatic utterances. The passionate urgency of Mark's message can help us to ask why worship in most congregations seems neither urgent nor passionate.

It seems to me that our worship is often designed to discourage strong feelings of any kind. Something about how we have allowed worship to be conceived in our time has discouraged preachers and people alike from drawing from the wells of passion, the deep places where love and hate, fear and faith, sorrow and joy uncomfortably co-exist. The further we move from both experiencing and expressing our feelings in worship, the more we become captive of our culture and undercut our own need to be in Christian community. More and more, many of us attend worship out of duty rather than desire and expectations of inspiration or consolation are increasingly lowered. Every now and then, thank God, these expectations are exceeded, and we leave worship feeling as if God has spoken to us directly. This is more the exception than the rule, but it is nonetheless a sign that even today congregations are not beyond the passion of a loving God.

What is so often true of congregational worship is all too often true of congregational study and education as well. The best part of educational programming in churches is invariably focused on children and youth, populations that certainly require preparation in the realities of the faith. Adult education frequently receives short shrift. A few of the faithful generally attend some kind of adult Bible study, but for the most part, adults who worship regularly at a church participate infrequently, if ever, in educational activities. The lack of enthusiasm for adult education in congregations could be because it is so often done badly. Or it could be because we have not made a case for needing any particular kind of education to be a Christian. What do we urgently need to know to be a Christian in our time?

For the Markan churches, certain kinds of learning would surely have been required to be a Christian. For example, Christians would have had to become intimate with the teachings of Jesus. They would have had to learn about resisting the dominant culture as a way of life. Similarly, they would have studied what to do if confronted by the zealots or by Roman officials. How and when to pray? For what could they count on in the household of faith? They would have explored what obligations and commitments Christians had to each other; how they were to prepare their children for a commitment to Jesus Christ; what the implications of this commitment were for their work; and whether there were things they, as Christians, were no longer permitted to do.

The urgency that Mark communicates makes training and learning a necessity for survival. Clearly in our contemporary congregations, we do not understand training or learning to have anything to do with our actual survival. Are there things that we as Christians really do need to know to survive in our time? Perhaps a discussion of this question would lead to a different agenda for adult education. Are there not some things we do need to know to function as Christians? For instance, what do we need to know about relationships, about sexuality, about dependence and addiction, about money, about suffering, about sin, about success and failure?

Mark's portrait of the church cannot simply be substituted for ours, but considering it can enrich our understanding of our situation and cause us to raise new or different questions. Mark's portrait certainly calls for a different worship life and a different educational ministry from what we currently have. Can these Markan pictures help us reimagine our own need? Can we use Mark to engage in a critical dialogue with one another about where we are and where we want to go in our congregations?

Questions and Exercises for Further Study

1. Read the entire gospel of Mark at one sitting, keeping in mind the image of the church as an alternative community. What new insights do you get? What kind of questions do you have? Discuss your questions and insights.

2. Make a list of what you would like to experience as a result of regular participation in congregational worship. Now compare your list with your actual experience of worship. Based on this list, what aspects of worship would you like to see changed?

3. Think of a time when the work and ministry of the congregation really came through for you. What happened and how did this make a difference in your life?

4. Think of a time when the church failed you in your need. What happened? Talk about it, if you can.

5. What does the success and/or failure of the church have to do with worship? What is the connection between worship and the success and/or failure of the church? Does this insight have any implications for how your congregation should be worshipping in the future?

6. What do you think you need to know to be a Christian today? Is your congregation providing this training? What is lacking? Do others feel as you do?

7. What issues or problems make you angry about life right now? Are any of these things on the adult education agenda in your congregation? If not, why?

CHAPTER III

Matthew:
Households of Justice

Social Setting and Historical Context

Many scholars believe that the gospel of Matthew was written toward the end of the second generation of the Christian church, around 80-90 C.E., in the city of Antioch, located in Syria, Rome's most strategically important eastern province.[1] Syria was a center of trade and industry with a population of approximately four million. By Matthew's day Antioch, the capital of Syria, was exceeded in size in the Roman Empire only by Alexandria and Rome. Matthew's small Christian households benefited from the process of urbanization that made Antioch such a large city and such an important center for trade in the Roman Empire.

Matthew's households appear to have been materially prosperous. While Mark appealed to the poor and the marginal, Matthew seems to be dealing with the middle and upper strata of society. Matthew's households were living through a transition from rural to urban culture, from the Aramaic language to Greek, from an ethnically homogeneous constituency largely of low social status to an ethnically heterogeneous constituency that included people of higher status, often more financially secure than earlier Christians.[2] Biblical scholar Robert K. Smith suggests that Matthew's households included

> many landholders, merchants, businessmen, and entrepreneurs . . . people who could appreciate the words on debtors and courts in (Matthew) 5:25-26, be startled by the suggestions regarding generosity (so unbusiness-like!) in 5:39-42 and the casual attitude toward sound financial planning in 6:19, be captivated by the dealer of

pearls in 13:45-46 and confounded by the logic of the landowner in 20:1-16, and would need the warning about the fate of those who have this world's goods but fail to share their resources with their brethren.[3]

The communities to which Matthew's gospel was addressed found themselves in a culture structured around households holding values very different from their own, and there was considerable conflict among the Christian communities about how to deal with the distinctly different social attitudes of these alternative groups. As a consequence of this tension, both predominantly Greek and predominantly Hebrew Christian-households existed, with tensions within each community over issues of status, rank, and power. When we think about Matthew's concern for order in the divided Christian community, then, we cannot think only in terms of Hellenist or Hebrew; we must consider additional nuances such as rural- or urban-oriented communities and social rank and social status.[4] Divisions existed among households and within them.

Although Matthew's households seem to have been prosperous rather than poor, poverty surrounded these congregations. In addition, poor people were clearly members of the various households. These house churches were city congregations with problems of poverty, home-lessness, and social dislocation not dissimilar to what we are currently experiencing in urban America. In fact, Matthew's gospel is focused precisely on what congregations should do about poverty. The primary task of the church as it emerges in this gospel is that of doing justice to the poor. For Matthew the church is a household of justice; this is his central image.

Exploring Matthew's Image of the Church

While the gospel of Matthew includes all of the material included in Mark, it has a different structure and feeling from Mark's gospel. Matthew has less a sense of urgency than Mark and is more concerned with demonstrating that Jesus is the final fulfillment of the Law and prophets. Some scholars believe, in fact, that Matthew's gospel—structured around five books, each consisting of a narrative and a discourse—is meant to resemble the five Old Testament books attributed to Moses.[5] Here is Matthew's outline:

Prologue: Genealogy, Birth, and Infancy (1:1-2:23)

Book 1
    Narrative: Baptism, Temptations, Capernaum (2:24-4:25)
    Discourse: Beatitudes and Justice in the House (5:1-7:29)

Book 2
    Narrative: Authority and Healing (8:1-9:38)
    Discourse: Mission to and from the House (10:1-11:1)

Book 3
    Narrative: Rejection by This Generation (11:2-12:50)
    Discourse: Parables of God's Reign for Householders
                     (13:1-13:53)

Book 4
    Narrative: Acknowledgment by Disciples (13:54-17:23)
    Discourse: House Order and Church Discipline
                     (17:24-19:1)

Book 5
    Narrative: Authority and Invitation (19:2-22:22)
    Discourse: Woes to the House of Israel and a Blessing for
                     Just Deeds (22:23-26:1)

Climax: Passion, Death, and Resurrection (26:2-28:20)

The meaning of this gospel comes into full focus in Book 3. Chapter 13 is the turning point of Matthew's interpretation of Jesus' ministry. In the previous two books, Jesus' attention has been directed to the Jews. Matthew presents him as the fulfillment of the Law and prophets, but he is increasingly resisted and criticized, with growing conflict between Jesus and the religious leaders. By the end of chapter 12, the members of Jesus' own family, and, symbolically, the religious hierarchy, have become outsiders and have rejected Jesus' message. The climax of this conflict and tension comes in 12:46-50:

While he was still speaking to the crowds, his mother and his brothers were standing outside, waiting to speak to him. . . . But to the one who had told him this, Jesus replied, "Who is my mother, and who are my brothers?" And pointing to his disciples, he said, "Here are my mother and my brothers! For whoever does the will of my Father in heaven is my brother and sister and mother."

Here is the theological heart of Matthew's gospel. Households of faith cannot be based on race, blood, status, or wealth. The new communities formed in allegiance to the power of Jesus are based exclusively on whether a person does the will of the One who sent Jesus. Jesus' new family is not based on kinship or tradition but on being obedient to God, on living a life that reflects the will of God.

Unlike Mark, Matthew presents a message that is quite understandable. Matthew is convinced that you can know the will of God. Not only can you know it, you can do it. The gospel is focused on seeking to make this clear to the households of faith struggling to live in this new reality: What does it mean to know and love God? You can know what loving God means in this gospel; it is focused on right relationship both in the households and in the way these households relate to the world. The relational focus in all cases is justice. Right relationship, doing the will of God, and being obedient to the teachings of Jesus—are all understood as part of the work of justice. The call of Matthew's gospel is to be a household of justice.

Precisely what it means for these households of faith to do justice is addressed in each of the five books of Matthew's gospel. In the discourse in the first book (5:1-7:29), the focus is on what makes for a faithful household. The beatitudes (5:1-16) describe the quality of life that would and should exist in a household faithful to God. The blessing of God comes to those who are poor in spirit, who mourn, who are meek, who hunger and thirst for righteousness, who are merciful, who are pure in heart. Blessing also comes to the peacemaker and to those persecuted for righteousness' sake. The house is likewise blessed if it is reviled and persecuted.

It is difficult to imagine that the households of faith in Matthew's time actually exhibited the quality of life described in chapter 5. More likely they were often quite the opposite—divided, seeking the favor of the society around them, hungering and thirsting for their own fulfillment, less than merciful to each other, and guided not by purity of heart but by narrow self-interest. The beatitudes are not a description of the reality of those households of faith so much as they are a challenge to them to become an obedient community, a house of justice. Book 1 closes with a challenge to those households:

> You are the light of the world. A city set on a hill cannot be hid. No one after lighting a lamp puts it under the bushel basket, but on the lampstand, and it gives light to all in the house. In the same way, let your light shine before others, so that they may see your good works and give glory to your Father who is in heaven (5:14-16).

In the discourse in Book 2 (10:1-11:1), the focus is on the household as an agent for mission and as a center of a new inclusive community. Here the disciples are named and sent out. This sending out reveals a deep tension that exists both in Matthew's gospel and in Matthew's households. The twelve are sent out with this charge: "Go nowhere among the Gentiles, and enter no town of the Samaritans, but go rather to the lost sheep of the house of Israel" (10:5-6). It would appear that there were deep divisions within Matthew's households over who was welcome into this new family of faith and who was not. Matthew confirms this exclusive focus on the Jews with the narrow assignment given to the disciples; it broadens as the gospel continues and concludes with the Great Commission (28:16-20) to go, not only to the Jews, but to all the nations.

This second discourse not only establishes the households as mission stations but also sets a standard or establishes conditions for the work that is to be done. The disciple is instructed to:

> Cure the sick, raise the dead, cleanse the lepers, cast out demons. You received without payment; give without payment. Take no gold, or silver, or copper in your belts, no bag for your journey, or two tunics, or sandals, or a staff; for laborers deserve their food (10:8-10).

This instruction is not a call to heroic self-sacrifice but a call to hospitality in community. The believer could travel light without worrying about food or lodging because he or she would be received by households with loving hospitality. According to Matthew, households were to receive a disciple as they would receive Jesus. As a matter of fact, when a disciple came to call, he came precisely to represent the presence of Jesus. The emphasis then is on the quality of love and compassion in the community more than upon sacrifice on the part of the individual disciple. The second discourse concludes with this promise to the households:

> Whoever welcomes you welcomes me, and whoever welcomes me welcomes the one who sent me. Whoever welcomes a prophet in the name of a prophet will receive a prophet's reward; and whoever welcomes a righteous person in the name of a righteous person will receive a reward of the righteous; and whoever gives even a cup of cold water to one of these little ones in the name of a disciple—truly I tell you, none of these shall lose their reward (10:40-42).

In Book 3 the discourse (13:1-13:53) uses parables to convey how and why the image of the reign of God is so important for the Matthean households. In this discourse Jesus issues an invitation to a new community and a new way of life that the coming reign of God both promises and symbolizes.

Matthew talks about the reign of God as the kingdom of heaven. The kingdom of heaven will be like a sower who goes out to sow (13:3-23), like good seed sown among weeds (13:24-42), like a treasure hidden in a field (13:44), like a merchant in search of fine pearls (13:45-46), and like a net that was thrown into the sea and catches fish of every kind (13:47-48). Jesus gives his disciples an interpretation of these parables, but Matthew's gospel implies that the readers—households of faith—will grasp the expectations the parables embody and fulfill them.

For example, Matthew has Jesus tell the believers that every scribe who has been trained for the kingdom of heaven is like a householder "who brings out of his treasure what is new and what is old" (13:52). This means that the households are to honor the old, the Mosaic Law and the prophets, but they are also instructed to honor the new which Jesus represents and brings. Much of the conflict in the early Christian church was precisely over how much "new" was enough and how the old related to the new.

Ultimately, however, the third discourse must be understood within the context of Jesus' question (12:46-50) about who were his father, mother, brother, and sister. The reign of God requires a new community where allegiance and membership are not defined by ethnicity, gender, social status, or former identity. The households treasure what has been received, but they honor the new family and community that emerge in and through the Jesus who is faithful to the One who has sent him.

The discourse in Book 4 (17:24-19:1) is a consideration of church order and discipline in a divided community.[6] It consists of a series of household codes concerning issues of rank and status. The disciples come to Jesus to ask who is the greatest in the kingdom of heaven (18:1). Jesus responds by summoning a child to come; he suggests that "unless you turn and become like children, you will never enter the kingdom of heaven" (18:3). Whoever becomes humble like a child is the greatest in the kingdom of heaven. No one is to have special rank or status in the household of faith. Equality should characterize relationships in the household.

Having established a new norm of collegial relationship for the community, Matthew next turns to ways his divided communities might reunite. They are to make a place for the alienated (18:10-14), embody a method of communal correction (18:15-18), and be aware of the power of communal prayer (18:19-20). They are to forgive each other seventy times seven (18:21-22) and from the heart (18:23-35). This is a call for a new social community where Jesus is Lord and where equality and forgiveness characterize life in and among households.

Although Matthew's households were undoubtedly divided and in conflict, it is clear that they were also being called to be united in heart and mind. Matthew expects that this call to a new community of inclusive love and energizing forgiveness can be realized. The call is not to an ideal beyond reach but to a community that is real and vital even if also sometimes conflicted, unforgiving, and narrow-minded. Ultimately, it is a call to rightly ordered relationships—a call to justice.

In the narrative at the beginning of Book 5 (23:1-26:1), the practice of justice as the measure of the household's obedience to God is put forward with eschatological urgency. When the final judgment comes, sheep will be divided from goats on the basis of how the poor and oppressed were treated. Households of faith will be measured by the degree to which they fed the hungry, visited the sick, clothed the naked, cared for the imprisoned. It turns out that not to take care of the poor and the needy is not to love and honor God (25:31-46).

If the households of faith had any doubt about the relationship between doing the will of God and practicing justice both in and beyond the faith community, the parable of the final judgment makes the connections painfully clear. The church is to be a household of justice and the test of that reality is always the household's relationship to the poor, the widow, the exile, and the prisoner. In contrast to Mark's emphasis on suffering, the stress in Matthew is on obedience: The household of faith is to obey the one who sent Jesus by engaging in right relationships with one another and with the world around them. Author changes to "justice."

What Matthew is calling for is not salvation by works—far from it. Matthew's plea is that salvation should produce good works, establish right relationships, and energize compassion and care. The households' practice of justice is a sign that their salvation is real and that their conversion is continuing.

Conversion in Matthew's view is not sudden and final but gradual and continual. The new communities called into existence because of Christ did not magically or suddenly become totally new. They were new in that they had aligned themselves with Jesus. Yet in this allegiance they continued to reflect old commitments, past habits, and former values. They struggled with issues of inclusion and acceptance. They struggled not to reflect the *paterfamilias* pattern of their society. They struggled not to organize their life around status and power. Yet at the very moment of this struggle their continuing conversion to the kingdom of heaven was occurring. Individual conversion was always in the context of social and communal reconstruction. From Matthew's perspective you cannot be converted to Christ aside from or independent of a relationship to a community of believers. To believe in Christ is to join a new social community from which to nurture, deepen, and demonstrate that conversion. To be in Christ is to be in a household of faith.

Matthew's portrait of the church begins and ends with households that are called to embody and practice justice. To be in Christ was for Matthew to be in a new social community where the world is reordered and life is redefined. Matthew called for a new collegial reality that based its membership not on ethnicity, gender, social class, or special status but on whether the will of the one who sent Jesus was carried out. Whoever did the will of God was Jesus' brother, mother, and sister—the new family connection for those who believed. This doing the will of God was a matter of establishing right relationships, of doing justice, both in the household and in relationship to the poor and oppressed of the world. To understand Matthew's picture of the church is to begin to understand the nature, function, and reality of households of justice.

Implications of Matthew's Picture of the Church

What implications does the Matthean picture of the church have for us in congregations today? To bring these implications into sharper focus, let's consider the important question of membership standards and expectations in Matthew's congregations and in ours.

What does it mean to be a member in good standing in a Christian congregation in the United States? Almost irrespective of denomination or theological position, to be a member in good standing in a contemporary Christian congregation means to attend worship from time to time and contribute something financially. That is the definition of membership found in the bylaws of most congregations.

These bylaws do not state that you must come 25 percent of the time or give five hundred dollars a year. They simply say that a member must attend worship at some time and contribute something. So technically a person could be a member of a congregation in good standing (that is, be eligible to attend and vote at congregational meetings, receive the sacraments, and have a voice in important issues facing the congregation) by coming twice a year and giving a few dollars.

As this standard makes clear, we have in many cases settled for the lowest common denominator with regard to congregational membership—minimal attendance and financial support—and it is costing us much more than we might think. By defining membership in congregations in this way, we have lost our ability to make demands on one another or to raise issues of accountability to the community of faith. Generally, to be a member in good standing in a congregation has very little to do with spiritual growth, biblical study, financial discipline, or righteous living. It has to do only with minimal attendance and non-sacrificial support. Such standards back congregations into a corner because there is no basis upon which we can ask for more of ourselves or of one another.

Similarly, there is a tendency for contemporary Christians to believe that membership in a congregation is more a "right" than a privilege or responsibility. I once proposed to a congregation that we adopt a policy of annual membership renewal; each year members would re-commit themselves to membership. To be a member of that congrega-tion in good standing then would have meant that each member rejoin each year. I also proposed that a covenant of discipleship be developed annually. Each person who renewed membership would indicate what she intended to do to grow spiritually during the coming year, or what kind of outreach or ministry she wanted to be involved in, and what kind of financial commitment she would make in the coming year. My intention was to raise the ante on the meaning of congregational mem-bership by forcing the lowest common denominator to a higher level.

I was not prepared for the level of resistance that my proposal re-ceived. The members of the congregation were not willing to consider such a change in membership standards. The resistance seemed to be based on the notion that church membership was an individual right; no one dare suggest that I did not have the right to come to the church on my own terms. Interestingly enough, the most active members of this particular congregation were as opposed to this change as were those least active. There seems to be a deep resistance in American Protestant-ism to giving any one person or community power to evaluate or judge our lives. In the case of the particular congregation to whom I had made my proposal, it seemed that the congregation wanted membership rights but without responsibility for that membership.

A low level of expectation among members and resistance to raising those expectations poses a significant problem for a congregation. How can we achieve more if we cannot expect more of one another? How are chronically low levels of morale and participation to be addressed? Are we doomed to this downward spiral because we are unable or unwilling to adopt a different standard of belonging? How can we engage in a new and transforming conversation about the meaning of membership in congregations without triggering automatic and paralyzing resistance?

Perhaps we need a new way of thinking and talking about issues of membership. Perhaps attendance and financial support are inadequate criteria; perhaps they need even to be abandoned. They are certainly not the membership criteria we find in Matthew's households. This is not to suggest that money and attendance are unimportant in Matthean house-holds, but they are by no means the primary standard for measuring membership.

The primary criteria for membership in Matthew's household is doing the will of the one who sent Jesus (12:46-50). One does the will of God by engaging in the practice of justice both in and beyond the household of faith. The focus of membership, then, is on the issue of right relationship with God, with others, and with the larger community. The standard is not perfection but commitment and engagement to struggle with questions of inclusion, forgiveness, compassion, and change. To do the will of God is to seek justice.

In our day it would seem that the practice of justice has little if anything to do with criteria for membership in congregations. What might happen if we switched the focus of membership discussion from norms of participation to norms of justice? I believe such a change would result in a different discussion, one brought about by a new definition of the problem.

To begin with, a consideration of justice as the primary criterion for church membership puts all participants on even ground. Too often a discussion of norms of congregational participation can encourage some to perceive themselves as more righteous than others. We can point to our attendance record with pride, or we can speak earnestly about tithing as "God's way" that surely everybody should choose to follow. But when it comes to the practice of justice and the establishment of right relations in our personal and social lives, most of us are more aware of shortcomings and failures than of successes, and rightly so. There is not much room for righteousness when it comes to the issue of justice. In fact, when justice is the criterion by which we measure our faithfulness, mercy suits our case and forgiveness speaks to our condition.

The issue of justice changes the conversation about congregational membership from one focused on what we do to one focused on what we are becoming. The issue of justice raises difficult questions with which we are forced to struggle. It helps us face our biases toward rich and poor. It asks whether we are grappling in our community with problems of inclusion and exclusion, or whether we have settled for a church based on common ethnic or class realities.

Justice is more difficult and complicated to discuss than attendance or financial support because justice pushes us to confront ourselves and one another in direct relation to the teachings of Jesus. What does it mean to be poor in spirit, to mourn, to be meek, to hunger and thirst after righteousness, to be merciful, to be pure in heart? In truth, we are not sure what these things mean; in Matthew, however, the expectation is that households of faith will grow toward such behavior in their quest to become places of justice.

This issue of justice positions us all on strange new common ground. We approach it with uncertainty and less than full clarity. Yet to pursue God's will through the practice of right relationship has rich and profound implications for us as individuals and as congregations. It makes me as an individual face my own hate, prejudice, narrowness, and ignorance. It also invites me to face my own desire to love and be loved, to forgive and to be forgiven, to accept and be accepted. It also makes communities come to terms with their collective need, for the practice of justice is not something that anyone can do alone. It demands participation in a community of accountability, mercy, and love; without this, we get lost on our own or discouraged by how hard the task is.

Imagine what it would mean if participation in a congregation were not so much about "wanting something from you" as it was "wanting something for you." To be in the church, to be in Christ is essentially to choose to seek to be a new (born again) person who struggles to grow into a life of love, justice, and mercy. It is quite exciting to consider that the congregation could be a place where we, along with our brothers and sisters, could openly struggle with our shortcomings, our blind spots, and our judgmental natures. In effect, the church would then be not the place where the good people go but a place where people who are seeking to be good—that is, just—go in order to keep on the journey of faith that they have chosen.

Could it be that we in congregations have not been asking enough of ourselves? By this I do not mean that we should adopt more strict rules but rather that we should have the courage to take up the problems and issues that plague our lives and our world. Why can't we discuss sexuality in the church? Why can't we discuss divorce? Why do we not put our racism on the table and examine it? That is, why can't the issue of right relationship be at the center of our worship, study, and practice as congregations? Do we not need help with our central relationships? How do we have partners, raise children, do meaningful work, love our neighbor, not be against people who are different from us, be merciful, and not grow cynical? How do we grow into the practice of right relationships expected in Christ and demanded by God? How can we possibly accomplish this without the support of a community of believers who are committed to the same journey and who care enough about us to tell us when we are wrong, hateful, or selfish?

For congregations to begin to answer this new question of justice
and right relation, clergy and laity alike require training far different
from what we have become accustomed to. Such training would stress
courage and openness in the pulpit, meeting room, and church-school
class. We might then face issues of justice and relationship as challenges
genuinely in need of exploration rather than as errors deserving correction. We need communal support to grapple with difficulty more than
we need quick fixes or easy answers.

As it moves toward its culmination, Matthew's gospel is unambigu-
ous about the final criterion to be applied to members of the households
of justice:

> When the Son of Man comes in his glory, and all the angels with
> him, then he will sit on the throne of his glory. All the nations will
> be gathered before him, and he will separate people from one
> another as a shepherd separates the sheep from the goats, and he
> will put the sheep at his right hand, but the goats at the left. Then
> the king will say to those at his right hand, "Come, you that are
> blessed by my Father, inherit the kingdom prepared for you from the
> foundation of the world; for I was hungry and you gave me food, I
> was thirsty and you gave me something to drink, I was a stranger
> and you welcomed me, I was naked and you gave me clothing, I was
> sick and you took care of me, I was in prison and you visited me."
> Then the righteous will answer him, "Lord, when was it that we saw
> you hungry and gave you food, or thirsty and gave you something to
> drink? And when was it that we saw you a stranger and welcomed
> you, or naked and gave you clothing? And when was it that we saw
> you sick or in prison and visited you?" And the king will answer
> them, "Truly, I tell you, just as you did it to one of the least of these
> who are members of my family, you did it to me" (25:31-46).

There is liberating potential for us in focusing a discussion of the
meaning of congregational membership on this depiction of the last
judgment. How exciting—the prospect of developing congregations
where the hungry are fed, the naked clothed, the stranger welcomed, the
sick comforted, and the prisoner visited! By becoming communities of
justice, we will of necessity practice the mercy and love depicted in this
story; in so doing we will find that we are ministering to Jesus and
becoming more and more like him.

but we Threw a boy rather than with for a members commitment to personal growth.

Imagine belonging to a congregation where justice and right relation are our primary concerns. While it is neither possible nor desirable to duplicate Matthew's communities, we will surely benefit from applying his picture of them to our present reality. In truth, our communities of faith have for some time now been deeply in need of a new picture of what it means to be a disciple of Christ. Matthew offers us such a picture; we have only to visualize it in our own day and begin moving together toward a new and more just world.

Questions and Exercises for Further Study

1. Read the gospel of Matthew, keeping in mind the image of houses of justice. How does reading with a concentration on this image change your understanding of Matthew?

2. In a month how often do you attend church? What percentage of the membership of your congregation is present in church on an average Sunday? What are the expectations of membership in your congregation?

3. How many new members did your congregation receive last year? How many are still active? What were they told about church membership when they joined? Who told them?

4. Is the practice of justice a part of your current membership expectations? Is there a way that inclusion of a concern about right relationships could change current practices? Would the issue of membership be different if you were talking about justice rather than attendance or money?

5. What would you like church membership to mean? What similar (or contrasting) ideas do other people in your congregation have about membership? Share your dream of what it means to belong to the church with someone else. How do they respond; what do they share in return? There might be more common expectations than you think.

6. What three issues about right relationships in your life or in the life of the church would you like to see discussed more fully in your congregation? Compare your list with another person's.

7. From your perspective, what are the three most vexing problems in your neighborhood or community? Do they affect the church? How? What contribution could the church make to a discussion of these issues?

CHAPTER IV

Luke:
Signs of the Kingdom

Social Setting and Historical Context

Luke's gospel was written from southern Greece between the years 80 and 90 C.E., toward the end of the second generation of the Christian church. It was directed toward men and women, most of them Greeks, who had been converted from some form of Roman religion or culture. By this time, Christianity had, for the most part, broken away from Judaism and was no longer identified as a Jewish sect; the households of faith were developing their own sectarian identity. Furthermore, the households had become a primarily gentile movement; increasingly their growth and expansion were a result of conversion to Christianity by non-Jewish residents of the Roman Empire.

Luke's gospel appears to be a response to several problems these churches were confronting as the end of the first century approached. The change from a Jewish to an independent sect was probably one such problem. It seems unlikely that the Christian households were legally recognized as a religion in the Roman Empire; rather, they were living on the edge of the law and subject to periodic persecution because of their lack of legal status. Luke's gospel may have been an attempt to establish the legitimacy of the Christian churches within the Roman Empire.

Then there was, as Fred Craddock has suggested, a need among these communities for a better sense of their own history.[1] What were Christians to do, now that the eyewitnesses to the life, death, and resurrection of Jesus were no longer present? By the late second generation of the church, the apostles themselves were gone. The imminent return of Christ had not occurred. The Lukan households were, more and more, being forced to rely on second-hand sources. Whether they liked it or not, the church was evolving on its own terms and being forced to stand on its own feet.

The community was, of course, guided by oral tradition, stories about Jesus, teachings ascribed to Jesus, and various interpretations of the meaning of the Jesus event. Luke, however, was concerned to capture the teacher's teachings in writing so that the developing communities of faith in southern Greece could more consciously apply Christ's teachings to their lives and the world around them. Specifically, Luke was concerned with the relationship between Jesus and the church's religious ancestor, Judaism, as well as with the evolving relationship between Jesus and the church. Because of the various changes confronted by the churches, Luke is the only one of the gospel writers to present a view of history that stresses the relationship between past and present.

In undertaking this task, Luke had the gospel of Mark as his guide. The entirety of Mark is found within Luke (both Matthew and Luke have Mark as a source). Luke also drew from other material that scholars often refer to as the "Q" source, using it to add additional detail and even content to the bare-bones outline of Mark.

Luke's aim in this undertaking was not to write a history so much as it was to write an interpretation of a historical event for the sake of the developing faith and life of his households. He was concerned about the question of the historical Jesus. Who was he? What did he do and say? What was the meaning of his death? What was the meaning of his resurrection? What mandate or mission did Jesus' teachings establish for the faith community? How did the early church develop?

Scholars have long held that Luke and Acts were written by the same person. The gospel of Luke asks and answers questions about Jesus and the Acts of the Apostles asks and answers questions about the development of the church. While we are focusing primarily on Luke's gospel, the connection between it and Acts sharpens our understanding of this first part of the Lukan corpus. As Fred Craddock has observed,

> Promise/fulfillment is a pattern characterizing the relation not only between the Old Testament and Luke but also between Luke and Acts. A few examples will suffice here. The reversal of fortunes

(mighty-humble, hungry-rich) sung by Mary (Luke 1:52-53) not only continued a social message in the preaching of John the Baptist (Luke 3:10-14) and of Jesus (Luke 6:20-26) but is the basic agenda for the ministry of the early church (Acts 4:32-37). And in the process the mighty were pulled down from their thrones (Luke 1:52; Acts 12:1-23).[2]

Patterns in both Luke and Acts, then, suggest that an important part of the social reality of the Lukan communities was a struggle, probably quite intense, over issues of wealth, power, and who was to be included in the Christian community. Luke's position on these questions is quite clear; his gospel stresses the importance of women, preferential treatment of the poor, and how hard it is for the rich to be saved.

All of these insights in Luke are organized around a central theme, that of the *basilea*, the kingdom of God. There are sixty-six references to the kingdom of God in the New Testament, and thirty-two of them are in Luke's gospel. This central organizing theme is Luke's primary image of the church: The church, the Christian household, is called to be a sign of the kingdom of God.

What does this central image of the kingdom of God mean in Luke? It means that, with regard to questions of poverty and riches, the weak and the strong, inclusion and exclusion, something utterly new is happening in the world. Mary's song (Luke 1:46-55) celebrates that "something new." In the birth of her child, a new reality is dawning. Mary magnifies God for "scatter[ing] the proud in the imaginations of their hearts" (1:51). God has

> brought down the powerful from their thrones,
>   and lifted up the lowly;
> he has filled the hungry with good things,
>   and sent the rich away empty (1:52-53).

The reign of God that Jesus both represents and announces is not business as usual. And the good news that Luke has to share with the churches begins and ends with this announcement of the kingdom of God.

Exploring Luke's Image of the Church

The structure of Luke's gospel is quite different from that of either Mark or Matthew. It is longer than Mark and moves with more spontaneity than Matthew. It has a highly narrative character, with Luke's stories about Jesus organized around the geographical locations of Jesus' ministry. One possible structure for understanding the gospel of Luke is as follows:

Preface: Luke 1:1-4

Part 1:   Infancy and Childhood Narratives (1:5-2:52)

Part 2:   Preparation for the Ministry of Jesus (3:1-4:13)

Part 3:   The Ministry of Jesus in Galilee (4:14-9:50)

Part 4:   The Journey to Jerusalem (9:51-19:28)

Part 5:   The Ministry in Jerusalem (19:29-21:38)

Part 6:   The Passion Narrative (22:1-23:56)

Part 7:   The Resurrection Narrative (24:1-53)[3]

After Luke introduces his gospel in the preface and Part 1, the meaning of the coming kingdom begins to be revealed in Part 2. Jesus is baptized (3:21-22) by John and immediately driven into the wilderness. "Jesus, full of the Holy Spirit, returned from the Jordan and was led by the Spirit in the wilderness, where for forty days he was tempted by the devil" (4:1-2).

Why did Luke feel it necessary to portray Jesus passing through this period of testing and temptation? The implication is that although Jesus had been baptized, he still was not clear about the direction of his ministry. Luke presents a period in which Jesus wrestles with what it might mean to announce the kingdom of God.

This temptation story functions as a vehicle for priority setting in Luke's gospel. The time of testing is spelled out in great detail. It is important to recognize that the temptations represent options or directions that Jesus could legitimately have chosen in the announcement of the reign of God. In the story, each option, referred to as a temptation, is rejected for a yet-to-be-specified plan of action. It would seem that Luke saw similarities between the drama of Jesus in the wilderness and the reality that his faith communities were facing; they too needed to go through a period of testing to be clear about the reality of the kingdom of God.

Consider the drama of this temptation story. Luke introduces the first test: "The devil said to him, 'If you are the Son of God, command this stone to become a loaf of bread'" (4:3). We might call this test the "economic option." One means by which Jesus could announce the coming of the kingdom is by feeding the poor and hungry. There were large numbers of poor people in Galilee who would have responded to such care. Jesus might have attracted a significant following by organizing his ministry around their physical needs. This was a substantive strategy that might have captured people's attention and been noted by the world at large. Jesus, however, rejects this option; he says, "It is written, 'One does not live by bread alone '" (4:4).

Then comes the second test:

Then the devil led him up and showed him in an instant all the kingdoms of the world. And the devil said to him, "To you I will give their glory and all this authority; for it has been given over to me, and I give it to anyone I please" (4:5-6).

This is what we might call the "political option." Jesus could introduce the kingdom of God by seeking a military or political solution. In Jesus' time, people suffered from the hardship of Roman occupation and might sympathize with any effort to overthrow the oppressor. This, after all, was the approach taken both by Saul and by David, two of Israel's great leaders. Longing for the restoration of Israel was part of Jesus' heritage, part of his formation as a youth in the synagogue. The political-military option with which Jesus wrestled was very much a part of his own history and spirituality. One way for Jesus to be the messiah, one way to announce the kingdom would be to become an earthly power bro-ker, a political leader, a king. In the end Jesus rejects this option as well: "It is written, 'Worship the Lord your God, and serve only him'" (4:8).

Then comes the third and final test:

> And the devil took him to Jerusalem, and placed him on the pin-
> nacle of the temple, saying to him, "If you are the Son of God, throw
> yourself down from here, for it is written, 'He will command his
> angels concerning you, to protect you,' and 'On their hands they will
> bear you up, so that you will not dash your foot against a stone' "
> (4:9-11).

This is the "miracle-worker option," the strategy of the spectacular.
Jesus might well attract a huge following by performing deeds manifest-
ing supernatural power. The dramatic, as we know, does capture attention and does bring crowds out to see what has happened. Jesus' announcement of the kingdom could have been enhanced by miracles that
take people's breath away. Jesus rejects this option as well, saying, "Do
not put the Lord your God to the test" (4:12).

By the conclusion of the story of the temptation in the wilderness,
we know what methods Jesus has rejected for announcing the kingdom
of God. We have yet to learn what strategy Jesus will employ, but we
know that he has struggled with several options and dismissed them as
temptations of the devil. The human Jesus, like the human community of
faith, had to search and struggle to discover the will of God.

Surely in these texts Luke is attempting to help his struggling faith
communities identify with the struggling Jesus. He is suggesting to the
households of faith that if the Son of God had to be tempted and search
for the truth, so would they. It was no simple matter to be a sign of the
kingdom of God. It was not an easy task for Jesus or the church to represent the dawn of a new age and give witness to the coming of a new
reality.

Following the three tests, Jesus returns to Galilee in the power of the
Spirit (4:14-15). He goes to Nazareth, his home town, and is invited to
the synagogue to read from the Torah scroll. He opens to the book of the
prophet Isaiah and finds the place where it is written:

> The Spirit of the Lord is upon me,
>   because he has anointed me to bring good news to the poor.
> He has sent me to proclaim release to the captives
>   and recovery of sight to the blind, to let the oppressed go free,
> to proclaim the year of the Lord's favor (4:17-19).

Here Luke reveals the results of Jesus' struggle with temptation in the wilderness. In fact, the remainder of Luke's gospel and the Acts of the Apostles are demonstrations of what has been revealed in this proclamation at Nazareth. It can be summarized as follows: The first concern of the kingdom of God is that good news should be preached to the poor. Jesus chooses to proclaim the kingdom of God by announcing that God has good news for the poor, the suffering masses. And in the gospel of Luke, this reference to the poor is to be taken literally.

The kingdom of God, moreover, is not only for the poor but also for the captive, the blind, and the oppressed. Luke's news of God's intervention begins at the margins, with the most distressed and alienated of men and women. The blind, the deaf, the maimed, and the diseased have a special place in the new reign ushered in by Jesus. Thus, in Luke the poor and oppressed are given preferential status. What Jesus intends in his fulfillment of the will of God is not to start at the top of society and work down but to begin at the bottom and work up. Such an approach, then as now, constitutes a reversal of the social order: What was down is now up; what was up is now cast down. The kingdom that Jesus both announces and represents turns traditional values upside down.

Why might Luke have announced the kingdom of God this way? Possibly because many of those in Luke's households of faith were on the margins of society, and this message was for and about them. Luke seems almost to be saying to the poor, "Do not forget that you are the purpose of the kingdom." To be poor or marginal was not, in this view, to be an inferior member of the Christian community but to be accorded a place of honor. This place of special honor given to the marginal is most dramatically portrayed in Luke's depiction of the resurrection (23:55-24:12), where the first witnesses to the event are women. Women, a group who had undeniably been on the margins of Jewish society and who were not even legally qualified to be witnesses, are entrusted in Luke's gospel with the good news of resurrection.

Luke also adds an economic dimension to Jesus' Nazareth-synagogue announcement of the beginning of the kingdom. The Spirit of the Lord was upon him, he writes, "to proclaim the acceptable year of the Lord" (4:19 RSV). This verse is a reference to the year of jubilee, the Hebrew practice of canceling debts every fifty years so that no one would become too rich or remain forever poor. This policy, outlined in Leviticus 25, was an attempt to regularize economic redistribution.

Whether the jubilee was consistently observed in Israel is doubtful, but there can be no doubt that the announcement of God's kingdom in Luke's gospel provides for redistribution of wealth and the forgiveness of debt. Clearly, the coming reign of God as portrayed in Luke's gospel includes and, in fact, emphasizes the importance of economics in the building of a new social order.

The option that Jesus announces in Nazareth is more complicated than those he rejected in his struggle in the wilderness. The passage Jesus reads, from Isaiah 61, was in the first century by no means a traditional text for understanding the coming of the messiah. Jesus gives messianic import to the passage by interpreting it to reflect both the nature of God's intervention and the program of action that was to begin that very day in Nazareth. With this announcement, Luke's Jesus calls into question the prevailing values of prosperity and success as well as more traditional expectations of what a messiah might do.

When Jesus finishes the reading from Isaiah, he sits down and declares, "Today this scripture has been fulfilled in your hearing" (4:21). The response from the members of the synagogue is sarcastic. "Is this not Joseph's son?" they say (4:22). Jesus then recalls two previous incidents in the history of Israel when God's messenger was rejected and God took the message to those outside the house of Israel (4:23-30). This causes such a storm of protest that Jesus has to slip through the crowd seeking to punish him for this bold proclamation. The good news that Jesus announces for the poor was received with anger in the synagogue.

For the households of faith Luke asks and answers the question of the nature of the kingdom of God by weaving together these two stories, the story of the temptations in the wilderness and the story of the proclamation in the synagogue in Nazareth. Luke's gospel makes abundantly clear that the households of faith are called to be signs of this kingdom.

Even in the late eighties C.E. such a contention would have been in direct conflict with prevailing social and religious values. The world then, as now, favored the rich, the powerful, and the influential. Luke challenged his faith communities not to be like the world around them. The church is to be a sign of God's reign and not a sign of the Roman Empire. The church is not to model itself after anything or any reality except the in-breaking reign of God.

In this gospel Luke is confronting what H. Richard Niebuhr has called a conflict between Christ and culture.[4] What is the appropriate relationship between church and society? From Luke's perspective the households of faith must not compromise their values to adjust or adapt to the values of the culture. Luke's depiction of the kingdom of God calls for resistance or even opposition to the dominant culture. To honor the kingdom of God requires that the households of faith have room for slaves, women, children, widows, and any others who are on the boundary of acceptability in the empire. Perhaps Luke was attempting to counter a tendency in the faith communities to become more legitimate in the eyes of the larger society. Perhaps some in the church were seeking to downplay the distinctive nature of the kingdom's demands. Perhaps some sought avenues of compromise in order to make daily life easier.

Luke's message was uncompromising: To follow Christ is to be a sign of the kingdom. The centrality of this theme is further explored in the litany of "blessings" and "woes" in the Sermon on the Plain (6:20-36). Blessing here is announced as unambiguously characteristic of the poor, and woe, characteristic of the rich. This passage contrasting blessings and woes is found, distinctively enough, only in Luke. Luke also depicts the appropriate Christian relationship to wealth in this new kingdom of God in the parable of the rich fool (12:13-21), the parable of the rich man and Lazarus (16:19-31), and the story of the rich young man (18:18-25), to name only a few.

While Luke repeats this theme again and again, one particularly powerful portrayal is the interchange between the imprisoned John the Baptist and Jesus (7:18-23). In this passage John, having doubts about the authenticity of Jesus, sends his disciples to him to ask, "Are you he who is to come, or are we to wait for another?" Jesus responds to this challenge not by defending himself or by making some traditional messianic claim but by pointing toward the dawning of the kingdom of God as expressed in events John's disciples were personally able to witness. Tell John, "The blind receive their sight, the lame walk, the lepers are cleansed, the deaf hear, the dead are raised, the poor have good news preached to them. And blessed is anyone who takes no offense at me" (7:22-23). In Luke, Jesus is indeed the one who is to come because the kingdom of God has come; the signs of that truth are that the blind see, the deaf hear, the dead are raised, and the poor have the gospel preached to them.

The incident with John the Baptist is a powerful restatement of the Isaian declaration in Nazareth. What was predicted is now visible. What was announced is now happening. What was foretold can now be retold. The kingdom of God is at hand; repent and believe in the gospel.

For Luke, the church was to be a sign of the kingdom of God. The faith communities, living out of the kingdom's power, were themselves called to do what was needed so that the blind would see, the deaf hear, the lame walk, the lepers be cleansed, the dead be raised, and the poor have the good news preached to them. The households of faith were to measure who they were by the same standards that Jesus used to report on his authenticity to John. The faith of the household was to be judged and evaluated by kingdom standards, not by Roman standards. In Luke, to be the church is to be a very specific sign of the kingdom.

Implications of Luke's Picture of the Church

To further explore Luke's picture of the church as a sign of the kingdom of God, I would like to consider the implications of this picture for the practice of stewardship in contemporary congregations. Can Luke's emphasis on the poor and his concern for economics help us to think about how we in the church get and spend our money?

One thing seems clear. Across Protestant denominations there has been a decline in revenues, a decline with primary impact on support to regional and national denominational organizations. As a result, virtually every mainline denomination has seen reductions in staff and cutbacks in services. More of the same is predicted. If factors of membership and attendance remain as they are, denominational leaders anticipate a continuing decline in financial support followed by even deeper cuts in services. The trend as we move toward the beginning of a new century is one of decline accompanied by a steady increase in the average age of our membership.

Similar economic factors are affecting local congregations. Congregations are facing declining resources and, at the same time, significant increases in the cost of pension and medical benefits for clergy. Congregations, even large ones, are spending more and more of their shrinking resources on salary, benefits, and maintenance. Mission is increasingly focused on survival with little remaining for outreach programs. If these trends continue, congregations with two hundred or fewer members will soon no longer be able to afford full-time pastoral leadership.

Part of the value of Luke's gospel is that it focuses on money. Luke makes money and our attitudes toward wealth legitimate topics for discussion. I find this refreshing because it is currently very difficult to have an open conversation about money in most congregations. Have you ever asked another member of your congregation the level of his or her salary? Generally the question goes unanswered or is ignored.

There seems to be some kind of taboo in most churches about talking honestly and forthrightly about such matters. Perhaps we are embarrassed to discuss it at all or are ashamed of how much or how little we make. I once asked a class I was teaching—primarily clergy—to write down how much they made a year and to share that with each other. They refused. There is something that makes money off-limits in most congregations. It would seem that you may ask people for money, but you must not ask them to talk about the meaning of money itself.

Luke's image of the church as a sign of the kingdom recognizes money as an ongoing problem for those who would be faithful; it declares that the poor are blessed while woe is coming to the rich. According to Luke, to be in the church is to "identify down" rather than to "identify up." That is, Luke is calling members to ally themselves in heart and soul and imagination with the economically poor, not with the wealthy.

The members of Luke's households are challenged to identify with the poor and needy, not with the rich and famous. As a matter of fact, if the believer's primary identification is with the wealthy and privileged, he or she is shut out of the dawning kingdom of God. The Lukan attitude toward wealth, with its predisposition toward the poor and marginal, is quite different from that found in most contemporary congregations.

In congregations today we do not, for the most part, believe that our common interests are with the poor and needy. Quite the contrary, we largely believe, or would like to believe, that we have more in common with people who are economically better off than we are. By adopting the values of this society, especially with regard to acquiring and consuming, we "identify up." We tend to believe, along with everyone else, that the answer to the question, "How much money do you need?" is, "As much as I can get." Most of us, that is, the vast majority of people in this country, are constantly bombarded by the media so that we will make common cause with those who have and define our self-worth by our ability to acquire what the merchants are selling. Most Christians long for the luxury auto, the perfect face, the expensive suit or dress, and those supersonic sneakers. In truth, in this culture you are "somebody" to the degree to which you possess and purchase. Our culture says, "Blessed are those who have" and "Woe to those who have not," but Luke says, "Blessed are the poor."

Congregations pay a high price for the spending habits of their members. Because we identify with those who have more than we and because we want what they have, we purchase our dreams on time. In my experience, a significant percentage of any congregation is deeply in debt by means of credit cards. Because the interest rates on such debt are quite high, many spend large portions of their monthly income servicing that debt. In truth, many Christians are tithing, but it is to Visa or Mastercard.

Luke's portrait of the church can help us in congregations to reclaim this issue of money as a legitimate focus of Christian faith and discipleship. Why should there not be an "economic" component to our discipleship practice and training? It may be that one of the chief reasons for tithing to God is to protect believers from consumerism. Money has such an impact on who each one of us is and what we are becoming that the question of stewardship cannot possibly be left to the individual. People need communal help to think through priorities, establish values, and make decisions with regard to this crucial aspect of life.

By attending to the use of money as it is understood in Luke's gospel, congregations have an opportunity to be and to make available an alternative to the dominant cultural value system. Perhaps we should develop a new evangelism around the very meaning and use of wealth in this society. Through teaching and discipline, congregations could become centers of alternative practice, centers of liberation from commodity addiction. Men and women could come to such congregations for help in considering what's really important, how to spend what they earn, and how to free themselves from the domination of a culture that seems increasingly intent on consuming itself.

In what ways might the church provide such an alternative to the values of our culture? Do we need to teach financial planning? Do we need to work on defining and modeling lifestyles that do not require unattainable amounts of money, lifestyles that help to generate new

, values? Should we take the lead when it comes to celebrating holidays such as Christmas and Easter? Do we need to establish our own credit unions? Do we need to think through what communal (congregational) economics might mean? Luke's portrait of the church at least encourages us to ask such questions and to evaluate our current practice.

There can be no doubt that the Lukan households of faith struggled with this reality. They also attempted alternative solutions to the problem. Acts indicates that the early disciples sold their possessions and goods and held all things in common (2:43-47). This radical form of economic sharing seems not to have lasted long; it does suggest an attempt to be an alternative to Roman culture. In what ways are we an alternative to American culture? Do we have any good news when it comes to what to do with money?

Imagine belonging to a congregation where you could get some help with thinking about money; where you could begin to understand why you tend to adore the rich and condemn the poor; where people would help you resist the pressure in this society to measure who you are by what you own or what you can buy; where you could talk about debt and what to do about it. Such practice would not be seen as the church meddling in people's private business but rather as the church giving appropriate and much needed care to some very difficult problems.

We need to face the fact that the problem of money and its meaning in our lives is probably going to get worse. It would appear that the young people now coming of age will be, for the first time in the history of this country, less prosperous than their parents. Many of our children will not achieve the level of comfort and success that some of us have assumed as our right. With a declining standard of living, fewer well paying jobs, growing national debt, and an uncertain economy, what will congregations do?

If we put ourselves in Luke's shoes, we will confront the issue of wealth directly and begin working to liberate ourselves from our addiction to consuming. We will deal with the whole person—head, heart, and pocket book. The time we are entering could be one of disheartening decline for congregations, or it could be an exciting opportunity for us to reclaim the initiative, charting a new and liberating course into the future instead of following along behind the values of this bankrupt culture.

Questions and Exercises for Further Study

1. Read the gospel of Luke, keeping in mind the image of the church as a sign of the kingdom. What new insights or questions does this reading bring to mind? Discuss your questions and insights.

2. How much money do you contribute to your congregation on a weekly or annual basis? Does this adequately reflect your commitment? Are other factors hindering you in your giving? What are they?

3. Evaluate your personal or family budget. Where does most of your money go? Are you pleased with the priorities that your budget reflects? Are there areas that you would like to change? Share this with someone in your group or congregation.

4. Evaluate your church budget. Where does the money go? Are you pleased with the priorities that the church budget reflects? Are there areas that you would like to change?

5. Do you think that many members of your congregation are deeply in debt? How might you find out and what could the church do to help?

6. What does your congregation do when someone is facing a severe financial crisis, such as the loss of a home or prolonged unemployment? What more could be done to pool resources and meet needs?

7. Design a course on good stewardship for our time, to be taught in one of the adult church-school classes. What topics would you want to see included, and what learnings emphasized?

8. Suggest a theme for a sermon on stewardship that you would like your minister to preach. What difficult issues should the pastor directly address?

Why education? – To make a good living not To be educated.

CHAPTER V

Paul:
Communities of Reconciliation

Social Setting and Historical Context

The earliest writings about the new Christian movement are attributed to Paul, who worked during the first generation of the church's development. Many of his letters were composed between 50 and 60 C.E.[1] Although scholars have varied and conflicting points of view about the Pauline letters, we know that Paul was one of the chief leaders of this new sect, which was a major influence in the church's movement beyond Judaism and in its rapid growth in the Greco-Roman world.

To understand the historical context of Paul's work, we must begin with his own conversion. Initially Paul was an opponent of Christianity. His efforts to persecute this new sect are recorded in his letters and in Acts. According to Acts, Paul participated in the stoning of Stephen (7:58), opposed the Christians in Jerusalem (8:3), and was traveling to Damascus to continue his persecution of "the way" (9:1) when he met Jesus. Paul's personal encounter with Jesus on the road to Damascus forever altered his life and work. It was a resurrection experience that resulted in Paul's designation as the apostle to the Gentiles (Acts 9:15; 22:21; 26:23; Gal. 1:15-16), and it was probably the prime factor in his decision to dedicate himself to this new way of life.[2]

Once Paul was converted, his mission to the Gentiles began immediately. Paul was by no means an idiosyncratic loner running around the Roman Empire shouting that Jesus was the new messiah. Rather, he was an urban organizer who, as he moved from province to province, was shrewd enough to use the most important cities in each area as his base of operations. He then sought the support of the churches already in each of these cities to underwrite his evangelization efforts. Sources tell us that in these operations Paul did not work alone but was the head of a team, probably involving forty to fifty people, women as well as men.[3] The travel and lodging of such an entourage would have involved considerable expense, expense routinely supported by the households of faith in the areas where the Pauline mission was taking place.

In the New Testament, Paul's letters are arranged in order of length, from Romans at the beginning to Philemon at the end. Several categories are used to group them. The travel letters were written during Paul's active ministry and include 1 and 2 Thessalonians, 1 and 2 Corinthians, Galatians, and Romans. The captivity letters, Philippians, Philemon, Colossians, Ephesians, and 2 Timothy, are those written from prison. Titus as well as 1 and 2 Timothy are usually called pastoral letters.[4]

The Pauline correspondence is marked by great variety. While some are personal notes or letters, others are highly public. While some go to households that Paul does not know at firsthand, others are addressed to communities near and dear to his heart. While several letters are pastoral in tone, with contents determined by the current needs of the addressees, one, at least, is clearly a rebuke and an argument.[5]

Some controversy exists as to which of these letters Paul himself wrote. Nearly all critical scholars accept seven of them—Romans, 1 Thessalonians, 1 and 2 Corinthians, Philemon, Galatians, and Philippians as written by Paul.[6] After Paul's death, his followers, sometimes called the Pauline school, continued to write in his name. These disciples of Paul are responsible for Colossians, Ephesians, 2 Thessalonians, and the pastorals.[7] It could be said that while Paul himself did not write all the Pauline letters, he was nonetheless their author. The passion, concern, and conviction of Paul shapes these documents and his character shines through the work of those who came after him.

Within the Pauline correspondence we find a rich selection of images of the church. The church is a new creation, the first fruits, the new humanity, the fellowship of faith, the people of the way, and the household of faith, to name only a few.[8] Two images of the church are central for Paul, however, and while one, the church as the body of Christ, functions as a basic ecclesial paradigm in Romans (12:1-21), 1 Corinthians (12:1-31), and Ephesians (4:1-16), the corollary Pauline image of members of the church as agents of reconciliation (Rom. 5:6-11; 2 Cor. 5:16-21; Eph. 2:11-21) will prove especially fruitful in our consideration of contemporary Christian congregations.

Exploring a Pauline Image of the Church

The Pauline households of faith are constructed on a primary foundation of the experience of reconciliation. For Paul, the reconciliatory event in all its power undergirds what it means to be a Christian, to claim Jesus as the messiah. Paul communicates to his households that something astonishing has happened in and through Jesus, and this "something" changes the very nature of being human. This experience of reconcilia tion appears as a central and powerful reality throughout the Pauline writings, but it expresses itself most clearly in Romans, Ephesians, and 2 Corinthians.

Paul understands reconciliation as a cosmic event that happened on behalf of an alienated and estranged humanity:

> For while we were yet weak, at the right time Christ died for the ungodly. . . . But God proves his love for us that while we still were sinners Christ died for us. Much more surely then, now that we have been justified by his blood, will we be saved through him from the wrath of God. For if while we were enemies, we were recon- ciled to God through the death of his Son, much more surely, having been reconciled, will we be saved by his life. But more than that, we even boast in God through our Lord Jesus Christ, through whom we have now received reconciliation (Rom. 5:6-11).

From Paul's perspective humanity was so severely estranged from God that God was moved to act on its behalf to overcome the great distance between them, that is, to reconcile them. The purpose of this reconcili- atory action in Jesus Christ is that humankind might no longer be strang- ers and enemies of God but friends and disciples (Eph. 2:19-20). This reconciliation in Christ is a tearing down of the "dividing wall" of hos- tility that separated humans from one another and from God (Eph. 2:14); it is an abolition of the law with its commandments and ordinances, in order to create "one new humanity in place of the two, thus making peace" (2:15-16). This new humanity that has been created in Christ makes the reality and ministry of reconciliation possible.

In the Pauline households, anyone who accepts this gift of reconcili- ation also receives a new power for life. For Paul, to accept the recon- ciliation that God makes available through Christ is to enter into a new kind of human existence, to become a new creation.

From now on, therefore, we regard no one from a human point of view; even though we once knew Christ from a human point of view, we know him no longer in that way. So if anyone is in Christ, there is a new creation: everything old has passed away; see, everything has become new! All this is from God, who reconciled us to himself through Christ, and has given us the ministry of reconciliation; that is, in Christ God was reconciling the world to himself, not counting their trespasses against them, and entrusting the message of reconciliation to us (2 Cor. 5:16-19).

Then, having been made new in Christ, these members of the households of faith receive the responsibility to extend this newness to others through the ministry of reconciliation. The task of the new creation is to form communities where the new can emerge, even if it does so in tension with the old.

There are at least three dimensions to the Pauline understanding of reconciliation.

First, reconciliation is personal. It is offered to men and women in the midst of their estrangement, alienation, and isolation. The same reality of Jesus that Paul experienced personally and directly is available to those others who would receive it. To be reconciled is to confront one's own personal need and come face to face with the forces that are at war within one's self. To be reconciled is to face one's own sin and be brought close to God.

This sin is not so much an act as it is a condition. That is, each of us is personally separated or estranged from God, but through God's initiative in Christ this condition is changed. Reconciliation in Paul's thought is the miracle by which this separation is overcome.

To be reconciled, to accept Jesus personally, is to adopt a new perspective about self, life, and God. It is a conversion from some old perspective to a new perspective, with Jesus and a new community as the center around which to organize personal identity and life purpose.

Think what an attraction this invitation might have been to first-century listeners. You are a displaced person struggling to make ends meet with no hope for any better future when you hear this strange new message about a messiah whose death and resurrection gives you a new status with God, a new human community, and a new personal identity. In the culture you are nobody or less than nobody, but in this new community, as interpreted by Paul, you are a loved and forgiven member of a new human family, a new creation. The rapid growth of this new sect suggests that the invitation extended by Paul and others to the Gentile world was in fact received as very good news.

The second dimension of the reality of reconciliation in Paul is social. While the first dimension involves a personal, though not a privatized, conversion, the second dimension focuses on social identity. To be in Christ is to take on a new social-political allegiance. Specifically, to choose Christ is to choose to be on the margins of the larger society. The process of reconciliation involves disconnecting oneself from the values and mores of the Greco-Roman world, after which the reconciled Christian adopts a set of values that enables the creation of a place for the stranger, the exile, the widow, the orphan, and the slave.

The experience of reconciliation involves a sense of being "over against" the dominant culture, for to be reconciled to God is to proclaim Jesus as Lord. Such an affirmation undercut the political authority of the Roman Empire because it put something and someone above the emperor and the state. For Christians to be reconciled to God and to one another in Pauline terms, they had to adopt a minority status both socially and politically, a status that made the church vulnerable to harassment and attack from political and religious authorities. Socially, the early Christians were near the bottom rather than at the top of Roman society, and this social location was fraught, at the very least, with some frustration and at times a degree of danger. Yet there was no gift of reconciliation apart from this new social identity.

The third dimension of the Pauline understanding of reconciliation is communal. To be reconciled in Christ is to be a part of a new community, the body of Christ. While, as we have seen, reconciliation for Pauline Christians was a personal experience, it was not a private matter, that is, it was by no means devoid of communal context. To be in Christ was to be a part of a new community that provided a structure in which to live out the new Christian social identity in the world. To be reconciled to Christ was to be a member of a household of faith where nurture, worship, education, and forgiveness were available. From Paul's perspective, reconciliation, both personal and social, was not possible without a communal context.

This communal dimension was the locus of some of the greatest difficulties for Christians who were actually trying to live out the new life of reconciliation. The emerging faith communities were often caught in a conflict between new gospel demands and old, familiar behavior learned prior to conversion. In Paul's communities, the call to reconciliation often involved a struggle that pitted the old against the new. And Paul's communications to many of the faith communities suggest that the old values and the old ways often got the upper hand.

While the invitation to reconciliation that Paul extended involved a new personal identity, a new social identity, and a new communal affiliation, it by no means guaranteed perfection in these matters. In fact, the radical nature of the invitation made struggles and difficulties almost certain. To become new is not easy work even if one wants this newness with all one's heart. The call to new life across the boundaries of class, gender, race, and need would certainly inspire as much resistance as cooperation. Such resistance to God's cosmic invitation to be reconciled to God and one another dwelt not only in the wider society, but also within each believer and in each community of believers. In effect, Paul's letters are a demonstration of the reality of reconciliation in progress. It was a work that was underway but was by no means complete.

The Pauline letters underscore both the radicalness of the invitation to reconciliation and the inevitability of resistance to this invitation by believers and unbelievers alike. Paul's disciples describe this resistance in terms of a battle: "For our struggle is not against enemies of blood and flesh, but against the rulers, against the authorities, against the cosmic powers of this present darkness, against the spiritual forces of evil in the heavenly places" (Eph. 6:12). As a result of this struggle, the community of faith is counseled to put on the armor of God so as to be able to withstand the forces of evil (Eph. 6:13-17).

Precisely because struggle is such an unavoidable part of the work of reconciliation in Paul, the establishment of communities is a crucial part of the church's ministry of reconciliation. The liberating content and works of the reconciliation event are impossible without a new community where love, forgiveness, and accountability can be experienced.

This trifocal liberation is what the body of Christ has to offer the world; the Pauline households of faith took up this challenge and realized it. At the center of Paul's vision of the church was a community of reconciliation. Perhaps this Pauline vision of reconciliation within the context of Christian community can help us to think creatively about late twentieth-century congregations as well.

Implications of the Pauline Picture of the Church

Benevolence and outreach is one aspect of congregational life and work
that needs consideration and rethinking in our time. What might the
community of reconciliation image in Paul's letters say to the traditional
"mission" commitment of congregations?

First, we will consider how Pauline communities of faith might have
understood outreach or missions in their context. Then we will examine
contemporary congregational practice more directly by looking at it
through Pauline lenses.

To begin, it would seem that what the early Christians had to offer
the world was themselves and their communities. They were not as a
whole blessed with wealth; neither were they in a position to have substantial influence in the reform of their society. In fact, the Christians, as
we noted earlier, were a tiny minority who lived on the edge of respect-
ability. Their mission was to share with others the unique experience of
reconciliation that they themselves had received.

This outreach work of the early church was to proclaim Christ as the
liberating messiah and invite people to convert to the power of that
reality. Christians invited people like themselves to give up what they
were and accept a new identity, the love of God offered in Christ. At the
same time, they offered a new, concrete social structure to belong to that
would strengthen and support that identity. Simply put, early Christian
outreach focused on creating the community we now call the church.

It is clear from New Testament sources that the early church did
engage in acts of charity and deeds of mercy. Acts describes the selection of deacons to serve the needs of the orphans and widows (6:1-7).
These acts of charity were, however, for the most part aimed at the membership of the church itself.

This intracommunity focus on the part of the early Christians was
not a selfish preoccupation with their own needs while neglecting the
needs of the neighbor, rather, it was a sign of the success of their outreach. The early Christian communities offered reconciliation with God
as an alternative to other ways of living in the world and people responded in significant numbers. The offer of a new personal identity, a
new social location, and a new communal membership brought orphans,
widows, slaves, and displaced and exiled people to the church in great
numbers. Deeds of mercy and acts of charity within the body were a
sign that the larger outreach was succeeding.

Being a community of reconciliation was itself the sum and substance of the early church's outreach. It invited people to come and share in an alternative perspective on reality and to participate in a new community where men and women, rich and poor, master and slave, Greek and Jew, able and disabled, all sought to live out the reality of this reconciliation. The very nature of such a community required that the community itself be the focus of mission and outreach. Certainly the early communities did not manage to deliver on all that they promised, but they promised a good deal more than do we in contemporary congregations. So we could say that they both failed and succeeded. Yet we must recognize that the attempt to create communities of such high expectation and alternative social formation was the heart of their outreach.

There must have been something quite compelling about the invitation extended by these households. The notion that life could be new, hates forgiven, and walls of separation overcome enabled ordinary men and women to create alternative communities; it gave them the courage to offer what they had found to others. The imperfection of their results should not surprise us. What is remarkable is that they tried to create such a new and different community at all. They actually sought to become communities of reconciliation.

What do these attempts to become such communities in the Pauline context offer us? Perhaps the Pauline perspective provides us with a fresh way to think about our situation. For when we look at the outreach and benevolence work of contemporary congregations, we see an exact opposite, a mirror image of the Pauline picture.

Would it be incorrect to observe that the current benevolence-outreach work of most congregations focuses primarily on acts of charity? The resources that we designate for outreach are generally given to places and organizations outside our congregational boundaries to reduce misery, support feeding or housing, or undergird the mission programs of our denomination. Few of our acts of charity or deeds of mercy are focused on our own membership. Outreach budgets focus on reducing suffering, improving the quality of life, and increasing opportunity or access.

Some may wonder what could possibly be wrong with such a focus. Don't millions of people, in this country and abroad, have real and compelling needs? Of course, and there is nothing wrong with helping the neighbor. Nonetheless, Paul's image of the church forces us to ask what our current emphasis on "charity" has to do with reconciliation.

In the New Testament, the trajectory of the Pauline communities was from the reality of reconciliation to a concern for acts of charity and deeds of mercy. Can we say that our benevolence-outreach efforts, expressed in acts of charity, move us toward the reality of reconciliation either within the congregations or in the wider society? Or have we, for the most part, abandoned reconciliation as a paradigm for understanding our outreach and benevolence?

Let's consider another way of thinking about benevolence. What if the chief thing we Christians had to offer the world were ourselves? Might the reality of an alternative community that invites men and women to join hands to overcome the hate, division, inequity, and violence that plague our world and our hearts be more important than deeds of charity or acts of mercy? Do we have something fundamentally new and exciting to offer our neighbors?

I should hate to give the impression here that I am opposed to us Christians caring about, helping, or loving our neighbors. Rather, I want us to think about the context of our caring and helping. Does outreach in our congregations focus fundamentally on the possibility of bringing about reconciliation between ourselves and our neighbors? Are we an alternative community of love and faith, and is this community our primary offering and outreach? Or are we, in our outreach work, primarily an adjunct of the social welfare apparatus of the state? Could it be that by thousands of us doing what we do, we unwittingly reduce discontent with the glaring problems of our society, and encourage people merely to get by? By taking some of the sting out of the needs of others, do we, in fact, participate in reducing the urgency of reconciliation?

Perhaps we need to face the possibility that we have let the practice of charity replace our commitment to reconciliation. Some may suspect here that to raise this question is to pit one necessary good against another. But I am suggesting that the context within which we think about what we are doing strongly influences what we actually accomplish. Reconciliation with charity at its center is a different vision of congregational outreach from the practice of charity as an end in itself, with little concern for the larger issues of social and personal reconciliation.

The practice of congregational charity, however sincere and well intended, can actually work against the reality of reconciliation. Many churches, for example, have set up shelters and feeding programs for the homeless. The need for such assistance is undeniable and overwhelming.

But do our efforts blur the larger questions of why there are so many homeless people anyway, and how the walls of hate, greed, and racism can be torn down so that a new humanity might be created? From a reconciliation perspective, we must concern ourselves with tearing down the wall of hate and division as well as with comforting the victims of those evils.

We have already mentioned another problem affecting current congregational outreach-benevolence efforts. With every year that passes, churches are being forced to work with fewer and fewer resources. Over the last decade, benevolence giving has been shrinking steadily in every major denomination, resulting in reduction of services and staff, if not outright elimination of programs. We are giving less to our denominational bodies and collecting less for outreach in our local areas.

This decline seriously affects our strategies for outreach. We are forced to cut back our support of worthy causes because we are paying more for housing, insurance, utilities, salaries, and so on. We find ourselves caught between the enormous needs of our society and ever shrinking resources. This reality of financial reductions and shrinking funds calls into question once again an outreach strategy based chiefly on the practice of charity. What can we do when we have less and less to give away even though more people are asking for the little that we have?

Added to these questions is the whole matter of understanding what seems to be a growing resentment on the part of many Americans toward requests for help from the needy. Is this tendency to withhold giving a sign of mean-spiritedness, of a growing disregard for the neighbor? Perhaps we in the church are, with many others in our society, growing less compassionate. Or perhaps the tendency to withhold expresses a deeper uncertainty about whether such giving responds effectively to our basic problems. There is, I think, a growing awareness that our problems are so large and complex that handouts, however well intentioned, do not help. Perhaps throwing spare change at our social and economic problems only makes matters worse.

The Pauline portrait of the church as a community of reconciliation challenges us to think anew about these problems and about how current congregational outreach practices do or do not respond to them. As we think about the mission of reconciliation, it may be that having less to give away will strike us less as a tragedy than as an opportunity. It may encourage us to offer ourselves as a community that calls for conversion

from the standards and values of the current age and invites women and
men to join us in creating a new community of love and forgiveness. Do
we, in fact, have anything better to reach out to our neighbors with than a
vision of life reconceived and reconstructed in Jesus, a life we are attempting, albeit imperfectly, to create in the community called a congregation?

We, ourselves, are the primary tool of our outreach. Have we
stopped inviting men and women to join our newly emerging humanity?
I am told that people do not want to join the church today, but I don't
believe that, and I suspect that you don't either. Men and women, our
friends and neighbors, still respond when they hear good news of the sort
that Jesus offers. An invitation to be loved, forgiven, and accepted is a
rare event for most people. The possibility of belonging to a community
of people working to reconcile the haters and the hated, those on the top
and those on the bottom, those who have and those who have not, the
citizens and the aliens never fails to strike a responsive cord. The very
event of reconciliation to God, to ourselves and to one another, or the
possibility of that reconciliation, is precisely what we Christians have to
offer.

As we invite friends, neighbors, and strangers to participate in the
miracle of healing, we will begin to experience in ourselves a deepening
of our conversion and a new appropriation of the miracle of reconciliation in our own lives. Inviting others to visit or join us very often puts us
in touch with the roots of our own reconciliation, our own calling to a new
personal identity, a new social location, and new communal commitments.
Could it be that we are reluctant to share reconciliation with others in
part because we ourselves have lost touch with the more elemental level
of our faith, the level at which we are called to be something entirely
new in the culture we inhabit? Perhaps we need a new conversion of
heart and mind in congregations in order to reach out and draw in men
and women who might join us, not in mirroring the values of our society,
but in creating an alternative based on forgiveness and love.

What might change in our congregations if we come to recognize
that the primary good we can offer the world is membership in a new and
reconciled community? At the very least, we would have to confront
within ourselves those practices and beliefs that keep us tied to old ways
and that make us more advocates for the status quo than for an alternative to the hate, narrow-mindedness, and inequity of our day. Focusing
on reconciliation might mean, for instance, that the homeless person

would join our community rather than spend the night in our shelter. We might bring the addicted into our congregation as well as support external treatment programs for him or her. Unemployed people might vote on the board of deacons instead of occasionally participating in employment programs that we sponsor or cosponsor. The same would be true of other people or groups struggling for self-respect and well-being. Think what a refreshing change it would be to be part of a community where the dividing walls of hostility were actually being confronted. Perhaps we should think of ourselves as being in the demolition business. That is, our primary task in congregations could be, not to make gifts of charity but, to tear down walls that separate us from God, from one another, and from ourselves. We must resist feeling helpless and passive about the walls of division currently marring our society and reach out to challenge and confront those forces of greed and hate that keep men and women from being reconciled to God through Christ.

Another way of conceptualizing this is to recognize that the basic outreach task facing us in congregations is to say "Enough!" to the evils that plague our society. We have had enough hate, selfishness, greed, injustice, and cruelty to last a lifetime. We are a community of reconciliation that has experienced another possibility, has been forgiven, and now reaches out to the world, calling forth the liberating possibility of reconciliation. Paul's picture of the church can help us to reimagine the nature of congregational benevolence and outreach in this way; it can enable us to engage in a critical dialogue about the nature of mission. Such a "job description" is not a utopian dream but an achievable vision, one we have every reason to begin working toward.

Questions and Exercises for Further Study

1. Read Romans 5:6-11; 2 Corinthians 5:16-21; and Ephesians 2:11-21. Discuss what Paul means by reconciliation. Apply this definition to your congregation. In what ways does your congregation resemble a Pauline community of reconciliation? In what ways is it quite different from such a community?

2. Make a list of all the "mission" or "benevolence" activities in which your congregation engages. How many of these help to build up a Pauline understanding of reconciliation in your congregation?

3. This book suggests that charity has been substituted for reconciliation in the outreach work of many congregations. Do you agree with this assertion? What difference does it make whether this statement is true or false?

4. What percentage of the funds your congregation collects goes for mission or benevolence? What does this reflect about the priorities of your congregation? Can it be changed? Has giving to mission declined over the last several years? What does that mean?

5. Is your congregation homogeneous according to race or class? Do you support works of charity for those different from you? Is it possible for your church to be a community of reconciliation while all its members are "alike"? How does the experience of being with people who are like you help or hinder your experience of reconciliation? What changes would you like to see in your congregation in order to deepen or broaden the work of reconciliation? What kinds of things might your congregation do to broaden its membership and reach out across current boundaries?

6. What kind of changes would be required for your congregation to become more diverse? Is there any support for such a change? Do you favor more diversity?

CHAPTER VI

First Peter:
Homes for the Homeless

Social Setting and Historical Context

The New Testament letter we know as 1 Peter was written during the reign of the Roman emperor Flavian (73-91 C.E.).[1] A general letter, it was composed in Asia Minor for circulation among the Christian households in the four provinces of that part of the Roman Empire. Scholars estimate that the population of Asia Minor during this period was 8.5 million with Christians totaling perhaps eighty-thousand.[2]

While much of the Christian movement examined this far has been urban in character, 1 Peter seems addressed to a primarily rural audience.[3] During this period, Asia Minor, in addition to being more rural than urban, enjoyed an enormous diversity of land, people, and local cultures, brought about in part by Roman efforts to urbanize the hinterlands of the empire. While these efforts were met with limited success, they did result in a large migration of workers within the region's four provinces as well as from beyond its boundaries.

From its beginning, 1 Peter has a very specific focus. Far from being addressed to the general population, it is written to groups of displaced people consisting of aliens permanently residing in Asia Minor or strangers temporarily visiting or passing through:[4]

> Peter, an apostle of Jesus Christ, To the exiles of the Dispersion in Pontus, Galatia, Cappadocia, Asia, and Bithynia, who have been chosen and destined by God the Father and sanctified by the Spirit to be obedient to Jesus Christ and to be sprinkled with his blood:
> May grace and peace be yours in abundance (1:1-2).

Some of these resident aliens were tenant farmers and migrant workers, while others were merchants, traders, and artisans. All, however, were displaced people far away from their homes. Even after their conversion to Christ, they remained aliens and strangers without a place of belonging or acceptance in the larger society. So the problem 1 Peter addresses is not one of "spiritual" estrangement and alienation. First Peter is not a theology of Christian exile, with heaven as its ultimate goal; this letter describes the real social conditions in which living men and women found themselves, and in which they worked out the implications of what it meant to believe in Jesus Christ.

The ethnic composition of the communities addressed in 1 Peter was mixed, consisting of both former Jews and non-Jews. By the time 1 Peter was written, new Christians drawn from among the Gentiles outnumbered Jewish converts.[5] The mixed composition of these Christian communities in 1 Peter probably reflects the mixed character of the population of Asia Minor itself:

> The vigorous flow of human traffic to and from Asia Minor was a . . . factor sustaining . . . heterogeneity. Commerce and trade by land and sea, entrepreneurial activities among the resident aliens from abroad, the attraction of educational opportunities (such as at the university at Tarsus) and health spas (at the renowned Asclepian springs shrines) and athletic and dramatic festivals, religious pilgrimages, mass movements of deported people. . . . all such occasions of movement to and from Asia Minor contributed toward the ethnic diversity of the peoples to whom and by whom the Christian gospel might be proclaimed.[6]

The resident aliens and transient strangers to whom 1 Peter is addressed also had a rather complicated social and legal status. Less than full citizens, they were generally seen as outsiders. In their time as in ours, outsiders were often targets and scapegoats for the social tensions and economic hardship of their area. First Peter's resident aliens were therefore victims of sporadic attack, not by the Roman Empire but by fellow residents of the region. The Christians of Asia Minor seemed to have been marginal and for the most part socially unaccepted. The break with Judaism probably made these social tensions even more pronounced because in the Roman Empire Judaism had received a certain social recognition and legitimacy that the Christian sect did not yet enjoy.[7]

Not surprisingly, the primary image of the church presented in 1 Peter is directly related to the problematic social situation in which the Christians to whom it is addressed—aliens and exiles, marginal and displaced people—find themselves. The primary image is that of the church as a household for the displaced. For Peter, the church is a home for the homeless. We now direct our attention to this image of the church in 1 Peter. What was Peter saying to the marginal and displaced Christians of Asia Minor about their mission and their future?

Exploring the Petrine Image of the Church

First Peter is a letter of encouragement and exhortation, consolation and confirmation (5:12). Given the difficulty that these new believers faced, it's easy to imagine their need for encouragement and consolation. First Peter is responding to some difficult questions that must have been on the minds of the believers of Asia Minor: Had their conversion to Christ brought any real improvement in their circumstances? Were they not, in fact, the same isolated and inferior aliens they had been before their conversion—as homeless and rootless as ever? Where was the community and acceptance for which they were yearning? How were they to contend with unbelieving husbands, wives claiming equality, or hostile neighbors? Why were they suffering? Why were they so slandered? Why did the Gentiles refer to them as "Christ-lackeys"? Why did they not experience more powerfully the grace of God and the certainty of their salvation?[8]

First Peter should be read with these burning questions in mind because one of the most helpful ways to understand this letter is to think of it as a strategy that responds to those questions, a strategy with three specific parts. First of all, 1 Peter seeks to emphasize that the Christian converts have a distinctive identity; second, it seeks to reinforce the internal power of their community; finally, it aims to explain plausibly the trials and troubles that afflict them.

First Peter is an exceptionally dense New Testament text and is not as familiar to contemporary Christians as a number of the other books we have been considering. I have chosen to present a fuller than usual outline with which to read this letter, one I see as highlighting both the questions raised by original readers of 1 Peter and the responses that Peter intends to these questions:[9]

Salutation: 1:1-2

Epistolary salutation—the apostle Peter to the elect homeless believers in the diaspora of Asia Minor.

Part 1: 1:3-2:10

By the mercy of God you strangers in society have become the elect and holy people of God, the household of faith.

A. 1:3-12

Praise be to God for the distinctive hope in salvation that we have through the faith in Jesus Christ!

B. 1:13-21

You, God's holy people, are to lead a distinctive, holy way of life in the hope of the revelation of God's grace.

C. 1:22-25

As a community purified through obedience to God, maintain your unity through constant brotherly love; for you have been reborn through a permanent word, namely, the good news of the Lord.

D. 2:1-3

Therefore avoid all acts of dissension and continue to feed on the milk of the word, namely, the Lord.

E. 2:4-10

You adhere in faith to the Lord Jesus Christ, the Elect and Holy One of God, through whom, by God's mercy, you have become the elect and the holy community of God, the household of the Spirit.

Part 2: 2:11-4:11

As strangers and resident aliens in society, through obedience to

God preserve the distinctiveness of the household of faith to the glory of God.

A. 2:11-12

As the elect and holy household of faith (1:3-2:10), live as holy strangers so that through your distinctive style of behavior even hostile outsiders ("Gentiles") might come to glorify God.

B. 2:13-3:12

Be subordinate and respectful to all human authority because of the Lord.

C. 3:13-4:11

Distinguish yourselves by the doing of good, even in the face of outsiders' hostility; God vindicates the righteous.

Part 3: 4:12-19

Rejoice in your suffering. Suffering for being obedient to the will of God is a distinguishing mark of your union with the Christ and of membership in the household of God.

Part 4: 5:1-11

Through responsible leadership, subordination, mutual humility, and resistance to the opposing forces of evil, maintain the unity of the community.

Conclusion: 5:12-14

Epistolary conclusion and greetings from the associates of Peter in Babylon.[10]

First Peter is addressed to households, the primary organizing units of the new Christian movement, spread across the four provinces of Asia Minor. Much of the letter is concerned with the qualities needed by these communities of faith in their relationships to each other and to an often hostile world. Given their status as wayfarers and aliens in the wider society, their task is to make homes for themselves and one another, that is, they are called to engage in the creation and sustaining of homes for the homeless.

Peter begins by responding to the discouragement and disillusionment of these communities of resident aliens and displaced people by reminding them of their status in Christ. Part 1 (1:3 through 2:10) focuses on conveying the new and extraordinary identity these new Christians have taken on through their faith in Jesus Christ. While the converts may have been displaced and denied respect in the larger society, in the household of God they are an elect and holy people. Peter declares boldly:

> But you are a chosen race, a royal priesthood, a holy nation, God's own people, in order that you might proclaim the mighty acts of him who called you out of darkness into his marvelous light.
> Once you were not a people,
>   but now you are God's people;
> once you had not received mercy,
>   but now you have received mercy (2:9-10).

In its entirety, 1 Peter seeks to reinforce the identity available to those who choose a new life in Christ. In effect, the convert receives a new home and a new reality. Perhaps in the larger society these believers are aliens, but in the house of God they are a royal priesthood. The believer's status within the culture is transformed through Christ and the church so that slaves are chosen, the displaced are holy, and the dispossessed are God's own. The initial phase of Peter's strategy for dealing with the believers' discontent and frustration is to remind them of who they are and to reinforce this new status and identity in Christ.

The second phase of the strategy employed by Peter in response to the needs of the church is to focus on the importance of maintaining a separate and cohesive community, one not assimilated or conforming to external social values.

Part 2 (2:11-4:11) challenges the believers to preserve the distinctiveness and solidarity of their households. They are to conduct themselves honorably among the Gentiles (2:12), do right so as to silence the ignorance of fools (2:15), not use their freedom as a pretext for evil (2:16), honor everyone but love only the family of believers (2:17). Holy lives in community will witness to their new status and will in time silence the voices of those hostile toward them. A tightly knit and separate community is critical to maintaining the momentum of conversion that has begun. Obedience is counseled as a way of both being like Christ and winning unbelievers to Christ (2:18-26; 3:1-6; 3:7). First Peter concludes this call to cohesive community with an admonition:

> Finally, all of you, have unity of spirit, sympathy, love for one another, a tender heart, and a humble mind. Do not repay evil for evil or abuse for abuse; but, on the contrary, repay with a blessing (3:8-9).

This maintenance of socio-religious distinctiveness, in addition to assuaging the sufferings of the displaced people of the households of faith, also was a necessary prerequisite for effective missionary witness to the "Gentiles" who abuse them and continually call them to account for the hope that is in them.[11]

The third part of 1 Peter offers encouragement and consolation to believers through a distinct perspective on the trials and sufferings these believers are experiencing. For this third aspect of 1 Peter's strategy to be grasped, Part 3 (4:12-19) should be read in light of two other portions of 1 Peter (1:6-9; 3:13-17), which also address the mystery of suffering. Thus contextualized, Part 1 invites believers to rejoice in their suffering because it makes them like Christ and assures them that suffering for God is never in vain. In this last age, trials test the purity and steadfastness of faith (1:6-7; 4:12). Suffering shows whose side the believer is on, God's or the godless "Gentiles" (4:2-3; cf. 2:17). Righteous suffering brings about unity not only with God and Christ but with the whole church (5:9). Endurance of the trials and sufferings by Christians occasions not grief and despair but "indescribable and glorious joy" (1:8, cf. 4:13).[12]

It was critical that the members of the households of God be able to make sense of their suffering. Meaningless suffering would soon weaken the households and threaten the very future of the small sect by leading toward assimilation and accommodation with the larger society. Peter's interpretation of the Christians' experience stresses the redemptive quality of suffering; it is precisely in their suffering that the Christians of Asia Minor are like Christ and, as such, will be strengthened and rewarded. At Peter's invitation, they saw suffering not as a curse or an unbearable burden but as a badge of honor, a sign of resistance.

This appropriation of Christian suffering as a means of strengthening the sectarian identity of the Christian communities in Asia Minor is a microcosm of the overall strategy employed in 1 Peter. By strengthening the identity of the believers, encouraging the power of community, and providing a rationale for suffering, 1 Peter reinforces the *oikos tou theo*u, the household of God, for the *parokio*, that is, for the aliens, the strangers, the dispossessed. According to this strategy, precisely because of the "nobodyness" of believers, their homelessness, their suffering and alienation, the church was able to be what it was called to be. The second-class citizenship of these aliens was not abolished by conversion to Christ; to be a member of the household gave a new meaning to this marginal status, a divine power, a sanctified purpose. Their exilic and displaced condition was given divine purpose, all of which was part of the divine plan for winning others, even enemies, to the good news available in Jesus Christ.

The image of the church in Asia Minor as a home for the homeless must have been quite a powerful one for it to succeed in maintaining such an identity over against the wider society. And clearly it did succeed. Men and women in great numbers joined, and together these new communities wrestled with living out the implications of this challenge. First Peter witnesses to the success and failure of this extraordinary attempt to raise up a church as an alternative to the evil that surrounded it, as a home for the homeless. This Petrine image of the church is, in fact, so powerful that it has as many implications for congregations in the United States today as it had for congregations in Asia Minor at the end of the first century.

Implications of the Petrine Picture of the Church

Like the images of the church we have already considered, the ecclesial image inscribed in 1 Peter—the church as a home for the homeless—can help us to reflect upon a variety of issues confronting contemporary congregations, social outreach or church membership, for example. At this time, however, I propose that we explore the implications of 1 Peter's image of the church for the understanding and practice of evangelism in congregations.

What did evangelism mean in the homes for the homeless that were the early Christian communities of Asia Minor? In truth, evangelism was at the very center of the identity and practice of these congregations. The church we find in 1 Peter is nothing less than a conversionist sect—a tightly knit community of primary identity with conversion as its aim. By constructing themselves as communities of solidarity offering a new social and personal identity to its members, these households at their very heart sought to be an alternative to the social and political options around them. Evangelism was their primary thrust. They wanted to live the good news that they themselves had experienced in Christ, of course, but they also sought to win over the opposition to this new way of life.

I find it interesting that the chief strategy these churches adopted for winning over the opposition, for attempting to convert "the Gentiles," was to be distinctly different from them. They consciously chose not to identify with the values and practices of their culture but instead created an alternative that offered men and women a choice. They did not "go along to get along" but maintained a distance from the norms and mores of society in order to make such a choice inevitable.

Membership in this new and separate community, this home for the homeless, was an intrinsic part of the good news these Christians offered in Jesus. This new community emerged out of protest and refused to accept the view of reality taken for granted by the larger society. It was radically egalitarian with membership for both slave and free, Jew and Gentile, male and female. It demanded a tremendous commitment on the part of believers and promised in return a new status in the human community and before God. Its good news came by virtue of these very demands, not despite them. These demands were the details of the contract of conversion, the substance of the evangelism experienced by the Christian convert.

What kinds of questions does this portrait of the church raise for our current understanding and practice of evangelism in congregations? First, we need to observe that conversion is not at the center of the work or experience of most congregations today. This is not intended as a criticism but as a description of our current situation. Congregations are posting considerably more membership losses than gains. This fact suggests that we are not for the most part converting members of the wider society to our way of life. Many mainstream congregations do not seem to use conversion as a category to understand their work. The more conservative or fundamentalist churches are those understood to be clearly conversionist in their perspective.

Is conversion then for us no longer an appropriate primary way of relating to those outside the church? In the Petrine community there was real and serious tension between the households of faith and the larger society. What today are the points of tension between the Christian community and the larger society? Or must we face the fact that the tension between the church and the world today has largely disappeared?

A major problem plaguing the church in our time is that its values and the values of the larger society are not markedly different from each other. And if this is so, if the tensions between church and world have been collapsed or at least lessened, then congregations have a real problem with evangelism. What is our good news? What is distinctively different about what we have to offer? What is deeply moving about the Christian life? Does our practice of love and justice reach out to others?

Evangelism assumes that good news is the essence of what we have to share in a world filled with bad news and old news. Are we still able to assume that? How many members joined your congregation last year? Were they really new members, or were most of them congregants' children doing what was expected of them? How many of your new members could be categorized as aliens, displaced people, or exiles from current society?

The image in 1 Peter, the church as a home for the homeless, implies that the purpose of evangelism is to establish and build up an alternative community, an alternative perspective on reality that is so compelling that people are drawn to it. Evangelism is not primarily about better planning, more skillful grouping according to class or color, improved public relations, or the latest in small group dynamics, though this is what much current literature on evangelism is concerned with.

Contrary to what many advocates of evangelism seem to think, the church's primary problem in relation to evangelism is not methodological; unfortunately, better techniques for evangelism will not bring us spectacular results. If we are to take the picture of the church in 1 Peter seriously, we have to face up to the fact that our problems involve, for the most part, not method but message. First Peter's picture of the church forces us to ask why congregations in our time have lost their distinctive edge and why we Christians have given up our unique identity and settled for being so much like the rest of the world. The solution to the issue of evangelism is not to adopt a new method or technique but to rediscover the urgency and meaning that separates being Christian from being American, white, successful, and privileged.

Consider your own experience in becoming a Christian and joining a congregation. Did you join that congregation because it was like everything else in your life? Probably not. More likely you joined because there was something different or distinctive that spoke to your life and concerns.

As I think back on my own life, it is quite clear to me that I was converted as a young person and joined a congregation because that small midwestern congregation was different from my world; the people of that congregation were different from the people I had known until that time. They reached out to me in my poverty and believed that I had potential. They, in their kindness and affirmation, offered me something radically different from the world that I lived in. What they offered me was such good news that I could not help but join them. With the congregation's encouragement, I began to dream about a future; I even began to make plans. By age sixteen I was preaching, with the support and instruction of my pastor, and was well on my way to a newly conceived life and purpose.

Isn't this precisely the meaning of evangelism, inviting people to engage in new life, to believe in themselves in a new way, and to experience the love that God has for them in Jesus' life, death, and resurrection? The church is not an adjunct to the wider society—like the country club, fraternal order, or PTA. It is an alternative community with a alternative perspective on the meaning and purpose of life, or it is nothing at all. When we lose our tension with the society, we also lose our good news and our distinctive offering. No wonder congregations are in decline.

Given the deterioration and need in our society today, is it not high time for congregations to reclaim their place as a home for the homeless? Could we not, if we chose to, offer an alternative to the consumer-oriented values of our society? Is not the vision of love and reconciliation at the heart of Christian community distinctly different from the values currently put forward by anyone else in this society? Surely we are aware of the suffering of our neighbors, ourselves, our local community? Is it not well within our potential to become a community of acceptance and compassion?

Our ability to engage in evangelism in congregations today is directly related to our willingness to stand back from the society and to separate ourselves from its values and practices. Once we take this distance, an alternative viewpoint and a new sense of identity will develop. Evangelism requires that we begin to separate from the values of our society so as to have something to offer in return. This is not, of course, separation based on some supposed superiority or need to condemn, but rather on an alternative identity for the sake of the world itself and the men and women in it.

One step contemporary congregations can take toward becoming homes for the homeless is to reclaim a strong sense of community. In recent times many congregations have come to look more like cafeterias than communities. In our desire to attract people, we have offered a variety of services or experiences that might please them, but we have not expected much back in return or asked for more than a minimal commitment. People have come and sampled these services—they've gotten married, had their babies baptized, and buried their dead with our help—without joining, supporting, or being changed by our community.

In truth what we in congregations have to offer is not a variety of services but an invitation to a new life with a distinct identity, a membership in a new community. A congregation is not like a bank, a fire or police department, or a welfare office. Our motto is not, "Call us when you need us." Rather, we are a community of men and women with a distinct identity seeking to offer people a place to work out who they are, what they are to become, as we seek together to be increasingly dependable and loving.

The formation and building of community is a critical component of our evangelism. Like our sectarian forebears, we are a protest movement with a distinctive point of view that does not find the status quo holy and blessed. We are seeking to understand life from the perspective of Jesus and to practice, however imperfectly, the love and justice that stems from Jesus' life, death, and resurrection.

This means that we understand that life is not at its center about acquiring and consuming, but about learning to forgive and be forgiven, to love and be loved, to overcome the bonds of hate and tear down the dividing walls of hostility—to create a new heaven and a new earth. We are seeking to paint an alternative picture of reality that has both a practical and an eschatological urgency. We want to be a home, a center of life and meaning for the lost, the confused, the exile, and the alien, the addicted, and the estranged. What draws people? The possibility of real community making available a new way of being. And this, at bottom, is what evangelism is about.

Imagine for a moment how attractive a congregation might be if it would clearly and intentionally provide an alternative community for your neighborhood. Of course, such a congregation does not appeal to everyone. It does appeal to those searching, however, to those in need, to those struggling with the meaning of their lives—people in our time who are much like the aliens and homeless addressed by 1 Peter. At this very moment there are such people in your congregation and beyond it needing an alternative community. Profound need and longing often go undetected and unconfessed in congregations because people often feel unsafe and unaccepted there. Within virtually every congregation there are alcoholics, addicts, physically abused spouses, adults and children who have been sexually abused, the divorced, people with various emotional and physical illnesses, and families who suffer with them. Within our very congregations are needs that can call forth a new community of compassion and acceptance.

Do we want to be an alternative community, a home for the homeless? The crucial question is not whether our congregation has the necessary contacts and connections to be such a community and, therefore, to begin growing again. We certainly do have them. The more important question is whether we have the will and desire to be such an alternative community of compassion and invitation. In the movie *A Field of Dreams*, the hero is told in a dream to build a baseball field in the middle of an Iowa cornfield. He's assured: "If you build it, they will come." As we set out to build our congregations into homes for the homeless, we can claim the same assurance: If we build them, they will come.

Questions and Exercises for Further Study

1. Keeping in mind the image of the congregation as "a home for the homeless," read 1 Peter carefully. What sections of this letter best embody this image for you?

2. In what ways is your congregation a community as it has been described in this chapter? What expectations of love or forgiveness exist among members? What other qualities of community characterize your congregation?

3. In what ways is your congregation like a social service agency offering various services to the unchurched or to marginal members? Do any of these services offer an opening for evangelism?

4. How much has your congregation grown over the last five years? Or has there been a decline? How are people invited to join your congregation? Are you satisfied with your current level of growth or is failure to grow one of the problems facing your congregation?

5. How could your congregation be more active in evangelism? How might you make a distinction between method and message as you consider the need for evangelism in your congregation? What factors or issues hinder your current evangelism efforts? What changes would you like to see in the way evangelism is currently done in your congregation?

6. If you were to develop a plan for evangelism in your congregation over the next twelve months, what would it include? Who would be responsible for it? What if any training for current members might it involve? Compare your plan with others in your group. Are there any similarities?

7. Discuss ways in which the concept of your church as an alternative community appeals to you. What would have to change in the life of your congregation for you to be able to think of your church as a "home for the homeless"? If it is not a home for the homeless now, what is it? What primary image of the church is currently operative in your congregation? Can or should it be changed?

CHAPTER VII

The Apocalypse of John: Communities of Resistance

Social Setting and Historical Context

The Apocalypse of John, also called the book of Revelation, was written at the close of the first century of the Christian church, near the end of the reign of the emperor Domitian (81-96 C.E.).[1] It, like 1 Peter, was addressed to the approximately eighty thousand Christians living in the four provinces of Asia Minor. Its author was a Christian prophet named John, probably not John the apostle but another leader-prophet of the early church known by that name. John wrote his apocalypse while he was under house arrest on the isle of Patmos and intended it for circulation among the households of faith throughout the region of Asia Minor.

To avoid the misunderstanding and misinterpretation that so often dogs this "last book" of the Bible, it is critical that we understand the place, time, and setting of its writing. Like the other texts we have been considering, the Apocalypse was not addressed to us in our time but to an actual group of Christians, in this case, Christians living in Asia Minor in the late nineties. Its purpose was to help them cope with the difficulty and suffering they were undergoing.

At the time of Domitian, the church in Asia Minor was, as we have discussed previously, a sect organized around households. It appealed primarily to those in the lower economic classes. Members of this new sect were widely suspected of being unpatriotic. Wild stories circulated about the cultic practices of Christian households. Some people believed that Christians engaged in a kind of cannibalism, eating the flesh and drinking the blood of Jesus. Others said they engaged in incest and orgies known as love feasts.[2]

John's apocalypse was a response to a crisis of identity experienced by many Christian households in the region of Asia Minor. As discussed in Chapter 6, these men and women were social outsiders subject to more or less constant tension and harassment, to economic and social discrimination, and sometimes even to the kind of mob violence reported in 1 Peter 2:11-4:11. It is only natural, in such a situation, for a group to question its identity.

The crisis of identity among these Christian households was caused not only by their marginal status in society, but also by Christianity's separation from Judaism, a process that had been underway for some time. By the last decade of the first century C.E., Christianity was an independent sect without recognition from or standing before the state. As a result, the households of faith were at home in neither the Gentile nor the Jewish world.

The book of Revelation was, in part, occasioned by this Christian identity crisis. As David Boring writes,

> "Who are the People of God?" and "What is the meaning of belonging to the church?" were not abstract theological questions but burning personal issues for John's readers, questions which helped shape the agenda of John's prophetic response.[3]

The text of Revelation seems also to suggest that John expected the Roman Empire to begin a systematic persecution of Christians momentarily. Three of the seven churches to which John writes had already undergone sporadic persecution: Ephesus (2:2-3), Pergamum (2:13), and Philadelphia (3:8-10). In addition, there was constant threat of persecution hanging over the faithful, and occasional actual incidents, although recent research suggests that no actual systematic persecution of Christians took place during Domitian's reign.[4] Boring helps us understand what these persecutions may have been like:

> A Christian or group of Christians is accused, from whatever motives, of engaging in illegal cultic practices and is brought before the Roman magistrate. Neither accuser nor judge understands very much about Christianity. The Christians are told they must prove their loyalty by offering wine and incense before the images of the Roman gods, including the image of Caesar. According to the

tradition which probably represents the actual situation, they were required to make the two-word acknowledgement of Roman sovereignty, *Kurios Kaisaros* ("Caesar is Lord"), an exact counterpart to the basic Christian confession "Jesus is Lord."

In addition they were required to curse Christ. We have documentation that those in later periods who complied were given a certificate exempting them from persecution. . . . Those who did not comply could be tortured or executed.[5]

The idea of declaring the emperor Lord was abhorrent to Christians, even if such an act would prove them good Roman citizens. Yet the imperial cult operative during the time of Domitian called for just such an affirmation, and the Christian communities lived under this threat, with all its attendant consequences.

Faced with growing pressure from the world around them to compromise and conform to the standards of Rome, the churches in Asia Minor were in crisis. John writes to help them to understand their situation and to work out an appropriate response. His advice is that these churches should resist evil with all their might; resistance is the primary mode of existence recommended to these churches. In fact, it is not too much to say that John challenges these households to adopt communities of resistance as their primary mode of self-understanding. We now consider the implications of this challenge for the church in Asia Minor.

Exploring the Revelation Image of the Church

An adequate exploration of the church as a community of resistance begins with a consideration of the genre, or literary style, in which the Revelation of John is written. Revelation is a work in the apocalyptic genre. As discussed in Chapter 1, one of the distinguishing features of the early church was an eschatological, that is, a future-oriented perspective on life.

Apocalyptic is a particular kind of eschatology. While all apocalyptic thought and imagery are eschatological—focused on the future—not all eschatology is apocalyptic. The apocalyptic genre is familiar in both Christian and Jewish literature and is used most often as a vehicle for communication in times of social and political crisis.

Apocalyptic thought assumes that a tremendous battle is going on between good and evil and that the believer is caught in the middle of this struggle. In the Revelation of John, apocalyptic thinking and imagery are used to portray God as the one who controls the meaning of history and its outcome. According to John, Rome may seem to have the upper hand, but actually God is in charge. Moreover, the end is very near, and the believer will be rewarded for endurance and resistance.

It's important to remember, then, that the primary question raised through the apocalyptic genre is not, "When will the end come?" but rather, "Who is in charge?" Such an interpretation of history encourages the politically powerless and oppressed to believe that God, not evil, holds power over creation. Accordingly, writers use the apocalyptic form to fire the socio-political imagination of the poor and the oppressed so that they will protest and resist. In general, the apocalyptic genre is used to create pictures and produce visions showing the contrast between good and evil and encouraging believers to understand the present through the lenses of a future vision. This is precisely the way John of Patmos used apocalyptic thought in Revelation to call forth protest and resistance from the churches of Asia Minor.

Revelation was designed to be read aloud and heard all at once in the context of worship (1:3). It must be understood as a whole and cannot be interpreted verse by verse. It is a narrative, a drama with action and movement that conveys the message of each part within the context of the total story. To pick out a verse or two and attempt to make sense of it apart from the whole is senseless and has led to endless distortion and misinterpretation of the book itself.[6]

The outline that we will use to understand the book of Revelation as a whole is as follows:

Letter Opening: Revelation 1:1-8

Part 1: God Speaks to the Church in the City (1:9-3:22)
    A. Transcendent Christ (1:9-20)
    B. Seven Messages to Seven Churches (2:1-3:22)

Part 2: God Judges the "Great City" (4:1-18:24)
    A. Transcendent God/Christ (4:1-5:14)
    B. Seven Seals, Trumpets, and Plagues of God's Judgment
       (6:1-18:24)
          Opening the Seven Seals (6:1-8:1)

Sounding the Seven Trumpets (8:2-11:19)
Exposé of the Powers of Evil (12:1-14:20)
The Seven Last Plagues (15:1-16:21)
The Fall of Babylon (17:1-18:24)

Part 3: God Redeems the "Holy City" (19:1-22:20a)
   A. The Transcendent God (19:1-10)
   B. Seven Scenes of God's Ultimate Triumph (19:11-20a)
     Return of Christ (19:11-16)
     Last Battle (19:17-21)
     Binding of Satan (20:1-3)
     Thousand Year Reign (20:4-6)
     Defeat of Gog and Magog (20:7-10)
     The Last Judgment (20:11-15)
     The New Jerusalem (21:1-22:5)
     The Vision Ends (22:6-20a)

Letter Closing: Revelation 22:20b-21[7]

    John writes this letter to the churches of Asia Minor (1:9-3:22) to equip them to understand what to do in a time of harassment and persecution. We must examine the picture the author is painting within this context, if we are to understand this visionary pictorial letter. With the larger picture in focus, the details involved in the various actions and judgments begin to make sense. What is this larger picture that the book of Revelation reveals?

    Two primary images form the center of the prophetic content of this book, the first, "Babylon," and the second, "Jerusalem." Following the letter's introductory sections, the opening proper, (1:1-8) and Part 1, in which God speaks to the church in the city (1:9-3:22), the letter focuses on God's judgment of the great city of Babylon (part 2; 4:1-18:24) and on the portrayal of God's new city, the New Jerusalem (part 3: 19:1-22:20a). Through this depiction of and contrast between the power, fates, and situations of these two cities, John instructs the churches of Asia Minor about their present and their future.

    What is Babylon and what does it represent? By the time John was writing, the ancient city of Babylon was a historical memory, not a living reality. For Jews and Christians, however, Babylon was a symbol of exile, a powerful enemy, and a place of humiliation and captivity. When John refers to Babylon, he is actually talking about Rome. John used the image of Babylon to describe the current realities of the Roman Empire and to discuss the future of that empire. Part 2 of the letter (4:1-18:24) is a vivid and graphic depiction of the evil of Babylon, the judgment that God was going to bring on it, and the fall of Babylon. The author spares no detail in his description of what was going to happen to Babylon and to those who conformed to its values.

The message of Revelation to the churches is that Babylon is doomed. It is a demonic reality that will meet its defeat before a holy and all-powerful God. God, the author promises, is working for the overthrow and fall of Babylon. As a matter of fact, when demonic Babylon falls, there will be great rejoicing in heaven:

> Then a mighty angel took up a stone like a great millstone and threw it into the sea, saying,
> "With such violence Babylon the great city
>   will be thrown down,
>   and will be found no more;
> and the sounds of harpists and minstrels and of
>   flutists and trumpeters
>   will be heard no more;
> and an artisan of any trade
>   will be found in you no more;
> and the sound of the millstone
>   will be heard in you no more;
> and the light of the lamp
>   will shine in you no more;
> and the voice of bridegroom and bride
>   will be heard in you no more;
> for your merchants were the magnates of the earth,
> and all the nations were deceived by your sorcery.
> And in you was found the blood of the prophets and of
>   the saints
> and of all who have been slaughtered on the earth."
>   After this I heard what seemed to be the loud voice of a
> great multitude in heaven, saying,
>   "Hallelujah!

> Salvation and glory and power to our God,
>> for his judgments are true and just;
> he has judged the great whore
>> who corrupted the earth with her fornication,
> and he has avenged on her the blood of his servants."
> Once more they said,
>> "Hallelujah!
>> The smoke goes up from her forever and ever"
>> (18:21-19:3).

Another city, the New Jerusalem, stands in contrast to the great city Babylon (Rome) whose fate is sealed and whose future is doomed. The New Jerusalem is the direct opposite of Babylon. Just as Babylon represents captivity, defeat, and exile, Jerusalem is the city of God, representing blessing and restoration. One author has contrasted these two as follows:

> Babylon is the city of death, Jerusalem is the city of salvation; Babylon, the dominion of alienation, babel, slavery, war; Jerusalem, the community of reconciliation, sanity, freedom, peace; Babylon, the harlot; Jerusalem, the bride of God; Babylon, the realm of demons and foul spirits, Jerusalem, the dwelling place in which all creatures are fulfilled; Babylon, an abomination to the Lord, Jerusalem, the holy nation; Babylon doomed, Jerusalem redeemed.[8]

Jerusalem, God's new city, is offered to the churches as an alternative vision in the midst of life in "Babylon." The churches, while they live in the reality of Babylon, long for and are sustained by the vision of the New Jerusalem. John portrays the New Jerusalem as God's promise to the beleaguered believers that history will end not in tragedy but in doxology, not in defeat but in dramatic restoration and redemption. While Part 2 of the letter describes the certain fall of Babylon, Part 3 describes the majesty and glory of the new city constructed by God and coming to all who were faithful to Christ and did not capitulate to the power of Rome:

> Then I saw a new heaven and a new earth; for the first heaven and the first earth had passed away, and the sea was no more. And I saw

the holy city, the new Jerusalem, coming down out of heaven from God, prepared as a bride adorned for her husband. And I heard a loud voice from the throne saying,

> "See the home of God is among mortals.
> He will dwell with them as their God;
> they will be his people,
> and God himself will be with them;
> he will wipe every tear from their eyes.
> Death will be no more;
> mourning and crying and pain will be no more,
> for the first things have passed away."

And the one who was seated on the throne said, "See I am making all things new." Also he said, "Write this, for these words are trustworthy and true." Then he said to me, "It is done! I am the Alpha and the Omega, the beginning and the end" (21:1-6).

This vision of the New Jerusalem was meant to be the power that enabled the believer to live in Babylon not as a captive but as a witness. The power of the future was to be a source of strength for enduring the power of the Roman Empire. As the households of faith wrestled with what it meant to be faithful to God in light of Rome's demands, the image of the New Jerusalem was a vivid picture of God's promise and God's power.

We can imagine the kind of dialogue that must have taken place in these Christian communities as they heard John's letter. Some surely wanted to quit. Being Christian was harder than they had thought it would be and was costing more than some were willing to pay. Others wanted to lie: Why not tell Rome what they want to hear but secretly keep Jesus in your heart? Others thought that an easier course of action would be to adjust the demands of the faith to be more compatible with Roman life and values. Why not compromise and adapt to make life more bearable?

In the midst of this dialogue and debate about what to do next comes John's prophetic challenge. John challenged the believer neither to quit nor to lie. The purpose of the vivid depiction of Rome as doomed and damned is to strengthen the believer's resolve not to take refuge in a reality that has no future. Rather, John counsels the believer to keep focused on God's future, the New Jerusalem. Do not adapt; do not compromise; do not bow your knee to this demonic and doomed power. The believer and the households are challenged to see a new day coming and to live in their time out of the strength of that new day. John wants to make it clear beyond question that God, not Domitian, is in charge, that God's power is ultimate while Rome's is temporary, that God will heal, reward, and sustain the believer while Rome's rewards cannot be depended on at all. At bottom, John is asking, "Who's got the power? Whose side are you on?"

In this passionate and powerful book, John calls the communities of Asia Minor to resist the evil that is so graphically embodied by Babylon. It is better to suffer and die, he tells them, than to compromise or betray Christ. The task assigned to the members of the communities of faith is to resist and help one another find the courage to stay faithful. The reward for successfully accomplishing this task is in the resistance itself, for those who do resist will gain citizenship in the New Jerusalem. "It is done!" John writes. "I am the Alpha and the Omega, the beginning and the end" (21:6).

Implications of the Revelation Picture of the Church

At first view, the picture of the church in Revelation as a community of resistance seems both frightening and confusing. Resistance has not been a primary mode of operation or behavior in Christian congregations for many years.

There was a time, of course, when the church sought to stand in tension with some of the values of our society. I remember quite vividly that when I was a young person, to be a Christian meant, among other things, not drinking, smoking, or dancing. As a matter of fact, during my teenage years members of my church would not eat in a restaurant where liquor was served. Also within recent memory Christians engaged in certain behaviors on Sundays that distinguished them from others—not going to movies, playing cards, or shopping. Some of these "signs of piety" are still practiced in some segments of the church, though they don't work for many of us anymore.

The Revelation picture of the church as a community of resistance helps us think about ways in which we Christians are different from the world around us and about appropriate contemporary ways of indicating what that difference might be. Put otherwise, it encourages us to recognize and examine our "Babylonian captivity." How are we, in fact, different from the larger society? Are there points of resistance at which congregations appropriately say no to the moral and political values of our society? How can we distinguish Christians from the rest of "the Americans" in this last decade of the twentieth century?

It can be difficult indeed to distinguish us Christians from the rest of "the Americans." Ties between the Christian church and American society have become quite close in our time. It is often difficult to tell where one set of interests begins and the other ends. Many people assume that there is a basic compatibility between God and country. Perhaps one of the clearest signs of this allegiance between church and state in our time is the presence of an American flag at the front of American houses of worship almost irrespective of denomination or theological tradition—a flag, standing right up in front of the church next to the cross, the communion table, and the pulpit. How might John have greeted a sign of the imperial cult in Christian houses of worship? The vision of the church that John's Revelation offers us can force us to consider critically our own captivity to our culture. Have we compromised to the point that we have diluted our witness?

John invites us to examine the degree to which we have become a civil religion used more by the state for its own ends than fashioned by us for God's ends. Our country is the largest arms merchant in the world. Our propensity toward violence is circling back to stalk us on the very streets where we live. We incarcerate a larger percentage of the population than any other nation in the world; well over half of these prisoners are African-American although African-Americans constitute only 10 percent of our nation as a whole. We invade a country like Iraq to protect our oil interests and feel no repentance when sixty to a hundred thousand men and women are killed by our intervention.

At home, we have built a fiscal deficit that is virtually guaranteed to strangle our grandchildren. We have allowed poverty and disease to grow to the point that our cities resemble some of the poorest urban areas in the Third World. More than a million men and women live homeless on the streets of America. The distance between rich and poor has grown at a shocking rate over the past decade. Today in the United States fewer than 20 percent of the population controls more than 80 percent of the wealth. Even those in the middle class are discovering that pensions and retirement benefits once considered sacrosanct are no longer necessarily secure. The "American dream" is far beyond the reach of countless numbers of our fellow men and women. Underneath much of this is a degree of hatred and hostility in American life that manifests itself in systemic mistreatment of certain symbolic groups—people of color, poor people, women, immigrants, Jews, homosexuals.

The prophet John thunders across the centuries to call contemporary congregations to resistance. Resist evil, he challenges; free yourselves from uncritical captivity, and honor the call of Christ. The application of John's vision to the actual situation of our society enables us to see what really is and to long for the not yet. John's vision of Babylon helps us to renounce idolatrous attachments to our society while his vision of Jerusalem draws us toward the new day we need, the one that most manifests what the church of Jesus Christ is really about.

One symptom of the church's current captivity to the society is the way in which clergy and laity are prepared for leadership in congregations. Today many seminaries, and many funding sources that support seminaries, place considerable emphasis on management skills, strategic and long-range planning, and financial skills. Millions of dollars have been spent in recent years to teach managerial skills to church leaders. What, you may be wondering, is wrong with that?

These skills, so highly stressed in the training of future church leaders, represent the basic orientation of many congregations toward our contemporary culture. They are primarily concerned with maintenance of the status quo. They focus on adapting, on making the best of what is given, without critically assessing the norms and values underlying this given.

Contemporary Christian leaders, lay and clergy, need skills in theological revisioning and analyzing the socio-economic situation confronting their communities far more than they need skills in adapting to that situation. These men and women need to learn how to build a new day, one that embodies a set of values and concerns different from the ones we have been living from. Why teach ourselves to make the best of what "is"? Far better to call into question what "is" for the sake of what is "not yet."

I am talking about the difference between a manager and a prophet. The church has, by my reckoning, too many managers and far too few prophets. That many of our seminaries cannot even imagine much less accomplish the formation of prophets is a concern worth worrying about. Neither do congregations, for the most part, encourage prophetic action or behavior. We have not been preparing our leaders, lay or clergy, to be prophets like John.

Can prophetic consciousness and action be taught? Certainly! Critical-prophetic skills are learned like any other. The capacity to look beyond the "now" to the "not yet" is an acquired skill not unlike time management or goal setting. What would happen if congregations were to understand their leadership training as the preparation of prophets? Even more broadly, what would happen if our adult education programs as a whole were reconceived as the formation of a prophetic community?

Comedian Flip Wilson used to say, "What you see is what you get." With this old quip we may begin to understand the difference between a captive community and a prophetic one. If in congregations all we can see is our current life with all its attendant problems, that life is precisely what we get. If in congregations we can see beyond the captivity of the moment to grasp the possibility of a future, then that in turn is what we get.

We need prophetic leadership if we are to break out of this tendency to adapt to the world as it is. The prophet, whether an individual or a community, is a visionary looking beyond what is given to see if there is more. The prophetic task is to keep one eye fixed on earth and the other eye fixed on heaven because you cannot create a future that you cannot see.

Revelation's picture of the church as communities of resistance challenges us to recover the power of the imagination. We need to teach one another to see what cannot be seen, to yearn for what is not yet, to long for what is not fulfilled. Part of this is giving ourselves in congregations permission to be disgruntled with what is as we develop our new picture of what God wants. Being disgruntled may be an expression of belief that God in fact does want something, wills something about the future.

We must let ourselves imagine the promise Revelation makes to us, that there is a new day coming in which there will be no more sorrow, pain, brokenness, division, hate, or enmity. Do we dare to believe this? Do we dare work for such a possibility? Do we dare hope that the lamb could lie down with the lion, that our spears could be beaten into pruning hooks, and our swords into plowshares? Could the new that God wills be a time of inclusion, forgiveness, and restoration? If the answer to any of these is yes, then we must resist every force that seeks to block, hinder, or delay the coming of this new day.

I believe that congregations can keep such liberating visions alive. Maybe congregations in our time are the very places best able to keep hope for a new future alive. I say this because, in my experience, every now and then, in spite of our captivity, we find our hearts warmed, our hope renewed, our sins forgiven, our limits stretched, and our eyes opened so that we catch a glimpse of another possibility. In congregations God does get through to us. We may have difficulty hanging on to the new, sustaining activity in that direction, but none the less we do see glimpses of that new day. Perhaps we glimpse it during prayer or singing or during the sermon or at work on a common effort, but, thank God, it does happen. Consider what might occur in congregations if we allowed these moments of vision to become more central and more expected?

Resistance is the spiritual discipline we need as we are poised on the threshold of a new century. We can begin to develop such a new discipline by giving ourselves permission to have questions, ask them, feel unfilled, long for more than life has given us, want to accomplish more than we have achieved, and set larger goals than we have previously dared to consider. We can also encourage the development of prophetic leadership by asking our pastors to speak more directly to issues that worry us and support them when they take risks. Many pastors would take more risks if they had more encouragement. Encouragement is infectious.

Prophetic leadership in congregations is also going to require the routine acceptance of a certain level of conflict. Not the grudge keeping and unresolved hostility that frequently characterizes some relationships in congregations, but rather the granting of permission for others to have different opinions. We need to listen even when we do not agree, to stick with conflict until there is some resolution or agreement to continue, and to outlaw personal attacks as unbecoming and destructive of prophetic Christian community. I know that dealing with conflict is not easy, but it is a skill we need to learn and practice if we are to become communities of resistance.

The Revelation of John may seem to us a difficult book, and it is. It is possible for us to understand it, however, if we are willing to struggle with the realities of Babylon and Jerusalem. In the contrast between these two visions, John's pictorial prophecies, judgments, and warnings begin to make sense. The churches in John's time received concrete help from this revelation. Those of us in contemporary congregations can, likewise, find concrete help for living if we are willing to struggle with our own Babylonian captivity and learn to long for the New Jerusalem.

Questions and Exercises for Further Study

1. Try reading the book of Revelation out loud all at one sitting. Stay focused on the larger pictures of Babylon and Jerusalem before seeking to understand the details of the various visions.

2. Do you believe that the church is currently suffering from a Babylonian captivity? In what ways?

3. How would you characterize your congregation? In what ways does it adapt to and compromise with society? What signs or acts of resistance do you see?

4. Is there any shared vision of a new future in your congregation? What is it like? Do you personally have a vision of the future? What is its source, and how do you nurture your vision?

5. Is there any prophetic leadership in your congregation? Do you encourage your pastor to be prophetic? How might you be more encouraging?

6. How might your congregation work on building a prophetic community? What might you change in your adult education, Sunday school, board, or vestry training to encourage prophetic consciousness and leadership from congregational leaders?

7. How do you handle conflict in your congregation? What do members fight about, by and large? What happens to the losers? Is learning how to disagree in Christ something your congregation needs to learn to do better? What concrete programs might be planned toward that end?

8. Make a list of what would help you grow spiritually. What would you like to learn to be able to imagine a new future, a new day? Are there portions of the Bible you would like to study? Do you need help with prayer? Are there theological books you would like to study? Compare your list with others.

9. From the lists of needs and concerns that have been shared, outline a Christian adult education program for the next six months that would facilitate the development of prophetic community in your congregation. How can you get this plan launched?

CHAPTER VIII

In Search of the Church: An Invitation

A Summary

For many years now it has been my conviction and my experience that congregations are capable of developing a new life much like the new life depicted in New Testament portraits of the church. Such a conviction has been the basis for this work. As you have explored the material presented in this book, I hope you have felt drawn to examine the life of your congregation. Congregations can and do make a difference in the lives of people, neighborhoods, cities, and, in the aggregate, even entire countries, and so it is crucial that we critically examine them and our notions about them.

The portraits of the emerging church in the New Testament are rich and varied. Each one examined here provides not only a description of the church in that early period but also a method for thinking about the church now. I challenge you to consider the implications for your congregation raised by each of these pictures of the church. What would it mean if your congregation regarded itself as a community of resistance or as an agent of reconciliation? What might it mean if your congregation's central self-identity was as a house of justice or a home for the homeless? What if the primary way you perceived yourself was as an alternative community or a sign of the kingdom? Later in this chapter there are some further suggestions to help you think about the redevelopment of congregations in this way.

There are three important dimensions to the redevelopment of contemporary congregations as depicted in the various New Testament images of the church. The first involves the development of human community. Christian churches in the first century represented a new way to be human and sought to provide a new social structure for that experience. To be Christian was to be a new kind of human being in a new kind of human community.

This daring creation of a new form of human community was perhaps the best and the worst thing about the early church; the best because such newness was so wonderful and so inviting; the worst because it was imperfectly realized and an inevitable source of disappointment. Nonetheless, the early church was, beyond a doubt, a new social structure making possible a new way of being human.

This notion of the church as a new human community can have startling implications for us in congregations today. Do we in our life and practice emulate this new creation? Do we encourage a new way of being human? What is the redemptive, barrier-breaking, life-giving dimension of our communal reality? Are we an alternative source of meaning and identity in our neighborhood or town? Does not the thrust of the Gospel as seen in the development of the early church call us to create alternative human community?

The second aspect of the New Testament invitation to congregational redevelopment involves resistance. Each portrait of the church that we examined depicts communities of men and women engaged in sectarian resistance. To be in Christ meant to be in some tension with the society as it was constructed, if not in open opposition to its values and mores. Resistance as a discipline of Christian life was a norm and not an exception.

I cannot help but believe that the reconstruction of Christian congregations in our day is intimately and necessarily linked with the recovery of a spirit of sectarian resistance. The call to oppose certain aspects of our society may make us quite anxious, but in truth the Gospel gives us little choice. We oppose certain things because we are Christians, even as our society supports or encourages them.

We have no choice, for example, but to oppose racism and sexism in any form. The Gospel leaves no room for ambiguity regarding such issues. In the body of Christ there is no place for hate, oppression, and the assignment of others to second-class status. Yet hate, discrimination, and oppression are normative in our society. What then are we to do? If we Christians were to begin by cleaning our own houses on such matters, think what a witness we would bear. Congregations will not experience new life without becoming painfully clear about what they support and what they are against. Until we deal with our own racism and sexism and stake out a position normatively different from the ones occupied by the wider society, new life in our midst will be a doubtful proposition. We have to give up the old to experience the new.

A third aspect of the invitation to redevelop congregations involves the recovery of eschatological thinking. Every New Testament community considered in these pages was characterized by some kind of significant focus on the future. Whether the early Christian households were described in Matthew or Revelation, in Paul or Mark, they enjoyed and cultivated a vision of the future that helped them make sense of their day-to-day struggles. The early Christians found courage to form new communities of resistance because they had a vision of what was going to be fulfilled by God, the kingdom that was yet to come, the new heaven and the new earth that was in preparation for them. The early church made a practice of seeing the unseen. By having a vision of the end, they were sustained in their struggles and inspired in their efforts to create the new even as they waited in eager anticipation for its coming.

This third aspect of the New Testament invitation to communal regeneration is critical. Our ability in congregations to form human community and to engage in resistance is intimately related to our ability to think eschatologically. After visiting hundreds of churches and talking with at least that many clergy, I have been forced to conclude that the church is undergoing a drought—a drought of the imagination. Very few pictures focusing on the future are being constructed in congregations. Too often there is instead exorbitant attention paid to the past, with a good deal of grumbling about the present.

We waste a lot of energy seeking someone to blame for congregational decline and depression. Much of the conflict in congregations today can be attributed to this imaginative drying up; because we cannot envision a future for ourselves, we are left to find fault with those who are at hand. I think you are familiar with this line of thought. If we only had a better minister, then _____. If we only had more committed members, then _____. And so it goes.

Can you see why a recovery of the ability to envision the future is important? We are stuck with what we have if we cannot see beyond it. Stuck is how many congregations feel; they do not like where they are nor what they have become, but they cannot see beyond themselves. If we could imagine a new future, we might be able to embody it or at least move toward it. Beyond a doubt, it is within our power to dream new dreams and have a new vision if we so desire.

I believe in thinking eschatologically in large part because I have experienced the fruit of such thought. I have seen the difference it makes when a congregation gets a vision about its mission. Consider, for example, a small store-front congregation of less than seventy-five members in Queens, New York, that became concerned about the number of hungry and homeless people in their neighborhood. Rather than complain about how bad things were, this congregation developed a vision of what they could do about the situation. They developed a picture of a future that involved a major effort to reach out to their hungry and homeless neighbors. This was something they had never considered and never done. Through prayer, conversation, sharing, hard work and with $2,800 in hand, this church in a recent year provided more than 10,500 meals to people in their neighborhood. What a new sense of confidence now permeates that poor store-front church and what exciting new relationships they have begun to develop with their neighborhood. This is not the same church that began to reach out; they have a new vision of themselves, new relationships with their neighbors, and a more inclusive community of believers.

When we consider how important a vision of the future is, I am also reminded of a dying white congregation in a residential neighborhood of a large eastern city. This church had declined to the point that fewer than thirty people were attending worship, most of them older adults whose families had moved away from what had become a racially changing neighborhood.

The members of this church were quite discouraged about the future until they began to generate a new picture of it for themselves. They realized that they had no future as an exclusively white church. They began to have a future, however, when they started thinking about what it meant to be the church, that is, to invite whoever was in the neighborhood to come. Their vision of the future changed; instead of being a white church in decline, they became an inclusive church open to the needs of the neighborhood.

First a Haitian prayer group came looking for a place to meet. Then a struggling Hispanic church needed space. Next a Chinese house church had outgrown its space and needed a new home. Before they knew it, this once dying church had become a center for multicultural ministry. The English-speaking congregation also began to grow. In less than five years a dying congregation of fewer than thirty became a growing, multilingual, multiracial church of more than eight hundred members.

What happened to them? Fundamentally, they got a new picture of the future. If you can see a new possibility, you can become it. At the center of the redevelopment of this one congregation was the recovery of eschatological thinking.

By now, I hope you are feeling some sense of excitement about possibilities for your congregation. Congregations can be redeveloped. New life can be experienced. We can form new and precious human community. We are capable of far more than we have achieved or have even dared to consider. The biblical pictures of the church that we have considered offer a variety of new ways to think about church contexts and to allow the power of the Holy Spirit to guide us. The real question is not "Can we be new?" but "Will we allow ourselves to become trans-formed?" In this sense, what happens in the life of congregations is up to each of us.

Next Steps

As an expression of the belief that more can be achieved in congrega-tions, this book concludes with two exercises. These exercises will, I hope, help you to synthesize insights derived from this material and move toward their application in your congregation.

Special note: It is important that one or two people take responsi-bility for these exercises, paying special attention to the exact timing of the various segments. Although I have suggested a certain length of time for each part of the activity, groups vary, and if participants begin to exhibit restlessness before the suggested time has elapsed, it may be a good idea to move on to the next activity. By the same token, during the discussion segment of the activity, resist continuing on to the next section of the exercise until participants seem to be finished saying what they need to say.

An Experience in Eschatological Thinking

This is an experience in visualization designed for use in a group. The group can be of any size, from four to eight to a hundred or more.

It is important that everyone have a comfortable place to sit and that at least an hour-and-a-half be set aside for this exercise. The experience is more likely to be successful if someone is chosen in advance to be the guide, keep track of time, and move the group through the several phases of the experience. This exercise is a good way to begin or end a retreat for church board members, leaders, or other church groups.

This activity, outlined as follows, helps members of a group to imagine a new future by visualizing the New Jerusalem of Revelation 21.

1. Sit comfortably with eyes closed while you listen to a selection of the hymns of the church. They can be taped or they can be played on the piano. This activity is not to be a sing-along but an opportunity to listen to the familiar to discover what images come to mind and what feelings surface. At the end of the period, each participant should reflect on whatever the hymns have called forth in memory and imagination. (Let the music play for fifteen minutes.)

2. Select someone in advance to read the description of the new heaven and the new earth in Revelation 21:1-6. It should be read for the first time just after the music has concluded and once or twice more during the following fifteen minutes or so.

While sitting silently, picture the kind of "new day" you would like. Be specific. What kind of images come to your mind? Who is in the picture? What are they doing? Can you hear anything? What feelings do you observe in yourself as you move through this visualization? Toward the end of this period, the leader should invite participants to jot down a few notes about their experience to share with others later. (Readings, silence, and note taking will take approximately fifteen minutes.)

3. After you have finished visualizing the new heaven and the new earth, switch your focus to the future of your congregation. While remaining silent, reflect on what you hope for your congregation. Picture what you would like your congregation to be in five or ten years. Once again, try to be quite specific in your visualization. What kind of people belong to your congregation of the future? What occupies them? How are they similar to your current community? How are they different? What feelings do you have about these changes and continuities? Once again, the leader should invite participants to make a few notes

about their visualization as a way of drawing this part of the visualization to a close. (Your mind should focus on your congregation for eight to ten minutes.)

4. For the next twenty to thirty minutes share with others in the group what you saw and felt. Each person might talk about the aspect of the visualization that moved him or her the most deeply. As each person shares his or her favorite picture, notice if a collective picture begins to emerge out of the shared experience of the group. What are the similarities between people's visions? Are some aspects of them apparently incompatible? If you are doing this in a large group, it is best to split into smaller groups of six to eight. Toward the end of the sharing, con-sider what implications for your congregation can be drawn from what you experienced. Is there anything further to be done with this information?

5. Spend the last fifteen minutes in prayer. Invite each person to express to God what he or she is grateful for as well as the needs each brings.

An Action Plan for Congregational Redevelopment

This second activity is a six- to eight-week process for congregational redevelopment. As few as eighteen and as many as fifty-four people can take part in it. It is especially useful as a method for involving the congregation in planning for its future. Leadership groups, such as the vestry, the board of elders, or the board of deacons, may find it useful for beginning such a process. (This exercise assumes that those participating have to some extent worked through the material in this book. Additionally, facilitators should be recruited in advance to help the process in each group move forward, paying special attention to encouraging everyone to participate and discouraging a few from dominating the process.)

Begin by organizing six working groups (three to nine in each group) around issues facing your congregation. These groups should not be constituted randomly, but should, if possible, be made up of people with interest, experience, or expertise in the issue under consideration. You may want to use the six issues discussed in this book (mission-outreach, evangelism, worship, Christian education, stewardship, and resistance) or adapt them to more precisely fit your situation. However you choose to do it, each group should focus on one issue. Here is a plan for organizing the process.

Week 1. Call together and organize the groups, announcing the plan to examine six focal areas of congregational life and develop proposals for the future of the congregation in each of these six areas. Each group adopts one issue and brings three New Testament pictures of the church to bear upon it.

After the issue groups have come together, ask members to choose three of the biblical images of the church explored in this book with the understanding that part of their task in the weeks to come will be to think through together the implications of these images for the issue they have taken on. If a group is to concentrate on worship, for example, group members might choose to examine worship from the perspective of Revelation (a community of resistance), Paul (agents of reconciliation), and Matthew (houses of justice). (Allow twenty minutes to half an hour for the groups to discuss the various images of the church and select the three they believe will be most helpful to them in their task.)

Additionally, at this first meeting the groups should agree about dates and places for future meeting. Below is a proposed timeline for the process:

Weeks 2-4: Each small group meets separately for at least two hours a week to discuss its issue, review and study its chosen biblical images of the church, and assess needs and concerns.

Weeks 5-6: Each group continues its weekly two-hour meeting, preparing during these three weeks a proposal for consideration by the congregation. This proposal on the assigned issue should address desired changes specifically, with particular attention to the steps—work, study, research, and consultation—necessary to implement it. Each proposal should be written in the context of the vision or visions of the church that it seeks to live out and honor. In other words, the plan of action that we propose is in service of what end?

Week 7: All groups meet together for a two-hour session to compare notes and exchange proposals. (Groups should be prepared to make multiple copies of their proposals available to one another.) Do not try to come to any conclusions at this session. Instead, each group should report on its process and share the record of its outcome. Facilitators should make note of and reflect upon areas of agreement and disagreement in preparation for the next and final session.

Week 8: In one final four-hour session with all groups participating, determine a plan of action in all six areas based on the six group proposals. Working together make a plan to move these proposals forward that will honor the results of your work. How much time is necessary for planning? For implementation? Who in the congregation needs to get involved in the next steps? Do we have some substantial points of agreement? Do we disagree? How will we handle this and move toward the future together?

At the end of the eighth week you may have charted out work for the next year or two. Whether anything happens beyond this initial process depends primarily on how well the next steps are planned and how much energy and commitment have been generated toward the issues that have been discussed. In my experience this kind of work generates a lot of new energy on the parts of leaders and members alike.

God's blessing on your next steps.

A Final Word

I bring all of this to a conclusion with the question of the psalmist on my mind:

> By the rivers of Babylon—
> > there we sat down and there we wept
> > when we remembered Zion.
> On the willows there
> > we hung up our harps.
> For there our captors
> > asked us for songs,
> and our tormentors asked for mirth, saying
> > "Sing us one of the songs of Zion!"
> How could we sing the Lord's song
> > in a foreign land? (137:1-4).

How do we sing the Lord's song in this strange land? Most likely, if we are going to sing at all, we will do it in the fragile and often unfaithful small communities called congregations. My hope is that the songs of Zion will pour out from our households of faith into the world where we, having recovered our identity, invite men and women into the joy of community, the power of reconciliation, and the grace of Jesus. Let's keep walking and working together, eyes focused on the New Jerusalem as we attend to the needs of the present. Our lives are important, our congregations life-giving, and our hopes will not be disappointed.

Chapter 1

1. For a discussion of Roman households in the first century, see Michael H. Crosby, *House of Disciples: Church, Economics, and Justice in Matthew* (Maryknoll, N.Y.: Orbis Books, 1988), 21-48.

2. John H. Elliott further discusses sectarianism in *A Home for the Homeless: A Sociological Exegesis of I Peter* (Philadelphia: Fortress Press, 1981), 74-78.

Chapter 2

1. Ched Myers, *Binding the Strong Man: A Political Reading of Mark's Story of Jesus* (Maryknoll, N.Y.: Orbis Books, 1988), 41. My thinking throughout this chapter has been guided by Myers's research on Mark, and I will be making frequent reference to it.

2. Ibid., 76-77.

3. Ibid., 83.

4. Ibid., 414.

5. Ibid., 164-66.

6. Ibid., 112.

7. Ibid., 117.

Chapter 3

1. My thinking is this chapter is strongly influenced by Michael H. Crosby, *House of Disciples: Church, Economics, and Justice in Matthew* (Maryknoll, N.Y.: Orbis Books, 1988).

2. Ibid., 39.

3. Quoted in ibid., 40.

4. Ibid., 41.

5. Ibid., 55.

6. Ibid., 70-72.

Chapter 4

1. Fred B. Craddock, *Luke, Interpretation: A Bible Commentary for Teaching and Preaching* (Louisville: John Knox Press, 1990), 17.

2. Ibid., 10.

3. Ibid., ix-xi.

4. See H. Richard Niebuhr's classic treatment of this subject, *Christ and Culture* (New York: Harper & Row, 1951).

Chapter 5

1. Luke T. Johnson, *The Writings of the New Testament: An Interpretation* (Philadelphia: Fortress Press, 1986), 249.

2. Ibid., 247.

3. Ibid., 249.

4. Ibid., 250.

5. Ibid., 251.

6. Ibid., 255.

7. Ibid., 255.

8. For a further discussion of the varied portraits of the church in the New Testament, see Paul S. Minear, *Images of the Church in the New Testament* (Philadelphia: Westminster Press, 1960).

Chapter 6

1. John H. Elliott, *A Home for the Homeless: A Social-Scientific Criticism of 1 Peter, Its Situation and Strategy* (Minneapolis: Fortress Press, 1990), 84ff. This is a primary source for my reflections on 1 Peter.

2. Ibid., 60.

3. Ibid., 63.

4. Ibid., 48.

5. Ibid., 66.

6. Ibid., 67ff.

7. Ibid., 69ff.

8. Ibid., 105.

9. Scholars doubt that the apostle Peter is the author of this letter. More likely, it was written by disciples of Peter and reflects the reality of Petrine leadership still being exercised in the early church even after his death. For a discussion of the authorship of this letter, see ibid., 270-79.

10. This is an adaptation of a fuller outline of 1 Peter in ibid., 234-36.

11. Ibid., 149.

12. Ibid., 142-43.

Chapter 7

1. This interpretation of the Revelation of John relies on M. Eugene Boring, *Revelation, Interpretation: A Bible Commentary for Teaching and Preaching* (Louisville: John Knox Press, 1989); and Elizabeth Schuessler Fiorenza, *The Book of Revelation: Justice and Judgment* (Philadelphia: Fortress Press, 1985).

2. Boring, Revelation, Interpretation, 11.

3. Ibid., 12.

4. Ibid., 17.

5. Ibid., 18.

6. Ibid., vii.

7. Ibid., 30-31.

8. William Stringfellow, *An Ethic for Christians and Other Aliens in a Strange Land* (Waco, Tex.: Word, 1973), 34.

The Alban Institute:
an invitation to membership

The Alban Institute, begun in 1979, believes that the congregation is essential to the task of equipping the people of God to minister in the church and the world. A multi-denominational membership organization, the Institute provides on-site training, educational programs, consulting, research, and publishing for hundreds of churches across the country.

The Alban Institute invites you to be a member of this partnership of laity, clergy, and executives—a partnership that brings together people who are raising important questions about congregational life and people who are trying new solutions, making new discoveries, finding a new way of getting clear about the task of ministry. The Institute exists to provide you with the kinds of information and resources you need to support your ministries.

Join us now and enjoy these benefits:

CONGREGATIONS, The Alban Journal, a highly respected journal published six times a year, to keep you up to date on current issues and trends.

Inside Information, Alban's quarterly newsletter, keeps you informed about research and other happenings around Alban. Available to members only.

Publications Discounts:

☐ 15% for Individual, Retired Clergy, and Seminarian Members
☐ 25% for Congregational Members
☐ 40% for Judicatory and Seminary Executive Members

Discounts on Training and Education Events

Write our Membership Department at the address below or call us at 1-800-718-4407 or 301-718-4407 for more information about how to join The Alban Institute's growing membership, particularly about Congregational Membership in which 12 designated persons receive all benefits of membership.

The Alban Institute, Inc.
Suite 433 North
4550 Montgomery Avenue
Bethesda, MD 20814-3341